C IS FOR CITIZENSHIP:

CHILDREN'S LITERATURE AND CIVIC UNDERSTANDING

by Laurel R. Singleton

Social Science Education Consortium
Boulder, Colorado
1997

ORDERING INFORMATION

This publication is available from:

Social Science Education Consortium
P.O. Box 21270
Boulder, CO 80308-4270

ISBN 0-89994-390-X

CONTENTS

INTRODUCTION

Then Miss Gates said, "That's the difference between America and Germany. We are a democracy and Germany is a dictatorship. Dictator-ship," she said. "Over here we don't believe in persecuting anybody. Persecution comes from people who are prejudiced. Pre-ju-dice," she enunciated carefully....

An inquiring soul in the middle of the room said, "Why don't they like the Jews, you reckon, Miss Gates?"

...Cecil spoke up. "Well, I don't know for certain," he said, "they're supposed to change money or somethin', but that ain't no cause to persecute them. They're white, ain't they?"

To Kill a Mockingbird, by Harper Lee
(Philadelphia: Lippincott, 1960).

This toy of voting was almost as pleasing as the conch. Jack started to protest but the clamor changed from the general wish for a chief to an election by acclaim of Ralph himself. None of the boys could have found good reason for this; what intelligence had been shown was traceable to Piggy while the most obvious leader was Jack. But there was a stillness about Ralph as he sat that marked him out: there was his size and attractive appearance; and most obscurely, yet most powerfully, there was the conch. The being that had blown that, had sat waiting for them on the platform with the delicate thing balanced on his knee, was set apart.

Lord of the Flies, by William Golding
(New York: Putnam, 1954)

Children's Literature and Citizenship

Works of children's literature can provide "compelling stories that invite students to identify with and care about social studies content" (Sage 1993). With the growth of the literature-based curriculum, social studies educators have begun reconsidering the role literature might play in developing young people's understanding of the social world.

McGowan and Guzzetti (1991) suggest several reasons why trade books can enhance social studies instruction:

1. Trade books are more readily comprehensible than textbooks, and they are available to suit a wide range of ability levels. Thus, trade books can increase the likelihood that all students will experience success in social studies.

2. Trade books are of high interest. Their engaging writing style and "sense of direction" make them more enjoyable than textbooks and therefore more likely to be read by students.

3. Trade books help students relate their own experiences to classroom content, a key factor in learning. Textbooks are rarely able to make these kinds of links between concepts and everyday experience.

Zarnowski (1993) also points out that while textbooks provide "brief and simple explanations of complex topics," literary works can be used to provide multiple perspectives and to show the varying interpretations that can be given to an event or idea. Because literary works engage students at several levels, Zarnowski also believes they can be a tool for encouraging in-depth exploration of social studies topics.

Furthermore, using children's literature can help teachers overcome their initial concern that concepts related to government and citizenship are too complex and abstract for young learners. Research indicates that learning at all levels—early childhood, late childhood and early adolescence, and late adolescence and adulthood—contributes to giving individuals the values, knowledge, and skills needed for citizenship in a democratic society. As Parker and Jarolimek (1984) have pointed out, "The emergence of citizens who are informed, skilled participants in democratic processes, and who are guided in their participation by a disciplined commitment to democratic values does not just happen as a result of ordinary living...political learning occurring in early childhood establishes the basic orientations of a person's political identity and the later political learning of adolescence and adulthood adds knowledge and skills. A foundation is laid in the early years on which a structure is later built."

Cautions in Using Literature in the Social Studies Classroom

This resource book is based on the belief that children's literature and citizenship education should be linked in elementary classrooms. The children's books mentioned are only a few of the many that could be used to develop civic understandings; our suggestions for their use are intended to serve as models. While children's literature can enhance social studies instruction, some cautions are in order. As Hepler (1988) has pointed out, activities developed around works of children's literature "should serve the reader and the book first, not some particular curriculum area. When the latter happens, *Charlotte's Web* becomes the basis for a science unit on spiders or a social studies theme of 'farming,' although to a child, the story may be about the power of friendship, or learning to stand up on your own piggy trotters."

Other cautions emerge from Levstik's observations of a class using literature as a vehicle for studying history. Levstik (1986) noted that "literature raises issues in an emotionally charged context." Thus, students need an opportunity to move beyond "their initial emotional response to an examination of the different perspectives involved..." Levstik noted that students tended to accept the information presented in literary works as "unimpeachable." In using literary works, teachers should therefore be vigilant about encouraging students to question the accuracy of the information presented.

Selection of appropriate materials is also a concern. In analyzing literary selections used in the K-3 texts of the Houghton Mifflin social studies series, Alleman and Brophy (1994) found some examples of effective uses of literature. They also, however, found examples of selections that focus on "relatively trivial or peripheral" aspects of social studies topics or goals, selections used in ways that trivialized the content (this was especially true when folk tales or myths were used), selections used to promote language arts goals rather than social studies goals, and selections that actually create misconceptions.

These problems highlight the importance of careful selection of literary works. Harthern (1993) suggests three criteria for selecting literary works for use in elementary history classes: the books should (1) have authentic settings, (2) involve realistic characters, and (3) reflect experiences, conflicts, and problem resolutions of the time. Alleman and Brophy (1994) suggest that teachers consider the following questions when selecting literature for use in social studies:

1. Does the source match the social education goals for the lesson and unit?

2. Does the source offer sufficient value as a source for social education content and a basis for social education activities to justify the social studies time that will be allocated for it?

3. Does the work seem to be of appropriate length given the social knowledge that needs to be included for adequate sense-making?

4. Does the work enhance meaning and not trivialize the content?

5. Does the work reflect authenticity and promote understanding of the content?

6. Does the work enrich social studies understandings as well as promote language arts or other subject-matter content or skills?

7. Does the source avoid potential misconceptions, unnecessarily shallow interpretations, or stereotypes in its depiction of people and events?

A number of sources are available to help teachers with the selection task. Annually, a National Council for the Social Studies committee, with assistance from the Children's Book Council, prepares a list of recommended children's trade books in the social studies; the list appears in the April/May issue of *Social Education*. Many of the books used in this publication were taken from recent years' versions of this list. Another journal of NCSS, *Social Studies and the Young Learner*, carries a regular column on children's literature and social studies. *Booklist, The School Library Journal, The Horn Book*, and the October issue of *The Reading Teacher* carry reviews of children's literature. These sources and such bibliographies of children's literature as *The Black Experience in Books* (Kirk 1993), *Guide to Children's Books about Asian Americans* (Blair 1995), *This Land Is Your Land: A Guide to Multicultural Literature for Children and Young Adults* (Helbig and Perkins 1994), and *Through Indian Eyes: The Native Experience in Books for Children* (Slapin and Seale 1992) can make teachers aware of high-quality literature useful in developing civic understanding. Many excellent web sites also provide leads for locating relevant works of children's literature. A great starting place is "The Children's Literature Web Guide" (http://www.ucalgary.ca/~dkbrown/index.html) maintained by David Brown at the University of Calgary. This site is an outstanding source with reviews, lists of prize-winning children's books, discussion groups, and scores of links to other children's literature sites, including sites of publishers who specialize in multicultural books.

Organization of This Book

This book has three major sections. The first provides a brief overview of five "big ideas" about government and citizenship that can be developed using children's literature. These understandings, which were adapted from the *National Standards for Civics and Government* (1994), are intended to help students develop a broad perspective on which they can later build as they learn more about the specifics of government and the rights and responsibilities of citizenship.

The overview of each "big idea" in the first section of the book is accompanied by suggestions for using works of children's literature to develop understanding of that idea. Some specific titles are annotated in conjunction with each idea. While the annotations include grade level suggestions, we recognize that every class includes students with widely varying reading skills. Thus, teachers may want to read annotations for other grade levels, may choose to read books aloud to the class, or may decide to make a range of books available for students to select themselves and then complete projects on. The suggestions for using these specific titles are generally brief. Keeping our first caution above in mind, the suggested activities are not intended to replace enjoyment of the books for their literary merit or their exploration of other important themes. Rather, they are designed to show how civic understandings can be developed through engaging activities that do not distract from the books' other merits.

The book's second major section provides guides for using specific works of children's literature to teach civic understandings. These guides are based on a format developed by Hepler (1988). Each guide includes a summary of the book, initiating (prereading) activities, discussion questions intended to stimulate critical thinking, and follow-up activities. The books included represent a variety of genres and are suitable for a range of grade levels. The guides are also cross-referenced to the civic understandings in the previous section of the book.

The final section of the book presents directions for three thematic citizenship education units based on children's literature. The first unit looks at the wide variety of forms of expression humans use and why freedom of expression is a basic value of American democracy, as well as an important right of citizens. In the second unit, students are exposed to diverse models of citizenship, expanding their understanding of what it means to be a good citizen. The last unit employs Kurt Vonnegut's story, "Harrison Bergeron," to stimulate student thought about the differences between *equality* and *equity*.

An index of the books mentioned in the text concludes the book.

Throughout the book, we have tried to provide examples for all grade levels, K-6. We have also drawn on a variety of literary genres, including picture books, realistic fiction, historical fiction, biographies, poetry, and informational books. Most of the books included were published since 1991, but a few are older. We make no claim that the books we have included are the best books for use in developing civic understandings. Many other works may be equally or better suited for these purposes. We hope that our suggestions will spark your own ideas for using other works.

References

Alleman, Janet, and Jere Brophy, "Trade-Offs Embedded in the Literary Approach to Early Elementary Social Studies," *Social Studies and the Young Learner* (January/February 1994).

Blair, B., *Guide to Children's Books About Asian Americans* (Brookfield, CT: Scolar Press, 1995).

Helbirg, A., and A.R. Perkins, *This Land Is Your Land: A Guide to Multicultural Literature for Children and Young Adults* (Westport, CT: Greenwood Press, 1994).

Hepler, Susan, "A Guide for the Teacher Guides: Doing It Yourself," *The New Advocate* (Summer 1988).

Kirk, Ersye, *The Black Experience in Books for Children and Young Adults* (Ardmore, OK: Positive Impact, 1993).

Levstik, Linda S., "The Relationship Between Historical Response and Narrative in a Sixth-Grade Classroom," *Theory and Research in Social Education* (Winter 1986).

McGowan, Tom, and Barbara Guzzetti, "Promoting Social Studies Understanding Through Literature-Based Instruction, *The Social Studies* (January-February 1991).

National Standards for Civics and Government (Calabasas, CA: Center for Civic Education, 1994).

Parker, Walter, and John Jarolimek, *Citizenship and the Critical Role of the Social Studies* (Boulder, CO: Social Science Education Consortium and Washington, DC: National Council for the Social Studies, 1984).

Sage, Cherryl, "One Hundred Notable Picture Books in the Field of Social Studies," in Myra Zarnowski and Arlene F. Gallagher, *Children's Literature and Social Studies* (Washington, DC: National Council for the Social Studies, 1993).

Slapin, Beverly, and Doris Seale, *Through Indian Eyes: The Native Experience in Books for Children* (Philadelphia, PA: New Society Publishers, 1992).

Zarnowski, Myra, "Using Literature Sets to Promote Conversation about Social Studies Topics," in Myra Zarnowski and Arlene F. Gallagher, *Children's Literature and Social Studies* (Washington, DC: National Council for the Social Studies, 1993).

USING CHILDREN'S LITERATURE
TO DEVELOP CIVIC UNDERSTANDINGS

Our purpose in encouraging you to use children's literature as a vehicle for developing civic understandings is not to have students read works of literature to glean facts about government. Instead, we recommend that discussion of literary works be focused on developing foundational understandings—"big ideas" that will provide a base on which students can construct more sophisticated and detailed understandings as they mature and are exposed to a variety of learning experiences.

The "big ideas" discussed in this chapter are based on the *National Standards for Civics and Government* but do not exactly mirror them. We have adapted the standards, dividing some into more than one big idea and omitting others. The adaptations are based on our analysis of which ideas can best be addressed using literature.

The following are the civic understandings discussed in this section:

Government: Government can be described as the people and groups with the authority to make, carry out, and enforce laws and to manage disputes about them.

Rules and Laws: Laws and rules are needed to guide behavior and establish order; laws and rules can be good or bad and can be changed.

Democratic Values and Principles: Our democratic government is based on values and principles in which Americans believe.

Citizens' Rights and Privileges: Citizens have rights and privileges that are protected by the Constitution.

Participation in Civic Life: Good citizens participate in civic life to promote the common good and to protect and improve our American democracy.

For each of these big ideas, we suggest a number of books that can be used to develop student understanding. Of course, many books can be used to develop several understandings, but we have chosen to illustrate each book's relation to a single understanding as a means of helping teachers generate teaching strategies around each big idea. For each book listed, we suggest grade levels for which it is suited—primary (K-2), intermediate (3-4), and advanced (5-6+). These suggestions are meant as just that; we recognize that the suitability of a book for specific students is best determined by someone who knows well those students, their interests, and their abilities.

Government

Government can be described as the people and groups with the authority to make, carry out, and enforce laws and to manage disputes about them.

Understanding government—what it is, what it does, where its authority resides, and why it is necessary—is a critical element of citizenship. As this "big idea" indicates, government can be described as the people and groups (i.e., institutions) with the authority to make, carry out, and enforce laws and to manage disputes about them. In a democracy, the authority or right to govern comes from the people—the consent of the governed. The authority to govern may also come from custom or law. Governments make and carry out laws and provide for defense, but different governments may carry out these functions in very different ways. Government is necessary to protect individuals from those who are greedy, selfish, or violent and to promote the common good. While government is both necessary and powerful, in our system, government is also limited. Government is limited by the Constitution and by adherence to the rule of law.

As the *National Standards for Civics and Government* suggest, young students can be introduced to these ideas through analogous cases of governance in the family, school, or neighborhood, cases that are common in children's literature. Because young children like to imagine how things would be different if they were in charge, picture books that deal with children's fantasies about ruling the world can also be used to develop this big idea. Older students can grapple with ideas related to government at the local, state, and national levels, ideas portrayed in both fiction and nonfiction, including biographies. Some examples of books useful in developing this big idea follow.

Too Many Tamales, by Gary Soto, illustrated by Ed Martinez (New York: Putnam's, 1993; primary), is an example of a family story that can be used to support this theme. Illustrated with luminous oil paintings, the book tells the story of Maria, who fears she has lost her mother's diamond ring in the tamales. She and her cousins eat all the tamales in a vain effort to find the ring, which turns up on her mother's finger. The four children's aching stomachs and Maria's embarrassment help illustrate some reasons why parents "govern" the family—to protect children from making mistakes and to safeguard the family's belongings.

Rachel Parker, Kindergarten Show-Off, by Ann Martin, illustrated by Nancy Poydar (New York: Holiday, 1992; primary), is a charming story of two new friends who find themselves competing over everything—who can swing highest, who can read best, whether having a cat is better than having a baby sister. When their competition leads to conflict, their teacher cleverly devises a situation in which they must cooperate to succeed. While reading the book, the class could stop right after Mrs. Bee tells Rachel and Olivia, "That's enough, girls." Students could discuss why the two girls are in conflict and what problems the conflict might cause for the class as a whole. They could also suggest actions that Mrs. Bee could take to stop Rachel and Olivia from fighting. They could then finish reading the story and discuss whether they like the strategy Mrs. Bee used and why they think this strategy worked. This discussion could be followed by a brainstorm of times from their personal experience that conflicts among young people were resolved by school "government"—teachers or administrators.

One girl's fantasy of ruling the world is presented in *If I Were Queen of the World*, by Fred Hiatt, illustrated by Mark Graham (New York: McElderry, 1997; primary). The queen's power (and self-indulgence) seem limited only by her love for her little brother, for whom she is willing to make some concessions. After reading the story, children could talk about the purposes of this queen's government, as well as limits they see on it. If they were queen/king of the world, what would they want to achieve (i.e., what would the purposes of their government be)? Would there be any limits on their authority? Why or why not?

Feathers and Fools, by Mem Fox, illustrated by Nicholas Wilton (San Diego: Harcourt Brace, 1996; all levels), is a powerful parable that—though a picture book—can be used with all grade levels to stimulate discussion of the need for government, as well as the dangers of prejudice and fear and the possible consequences of an arms race. The swans and peacocks live near each other but do not communicate. Instead, they let their fear drive them to stockpile weapons made from sharpened feathers. A mistake triggers a bloody battle that leaves all the birds dead. When a young swan and a baby peacock hatch from two eggs left behind, they see only their similarities and decide to be friends. The messages of this disturbing story are multileveled and should provoke much discussion. One focus of follow-up discussion could be: How could this disaster have been avoided? How could the two groups have worked together to more effectively provide for the "common defense" of their people, one of the purposes of government?

The purposes and functions of government are presented in a uniquely understandable way by Peter Spier in *We the People: The Constitution of the United States of America* (Garden City, NJ: Doubleday, 1987; intermediate, advanced). Following a four-page overview of the Constitutional Convention and the ratification process, Spier illustrates each phrase in the Preamble to the Constitution in a way that makes its meaning come alive. For example, for the phrase "insure domestic tranquillity," Spier presents 16 drawings illustrating how the government protects the safety of Americans past and present. Illustrating the phrase, "promote the General Welfare" are drawings of a mail truck, a TVA dam, a Veterans Administration hospital, a library, a Social Security card, weather balloons, and a national park, among many others. Because the drawings are quite small and detailed, students need the opportunity to examine them closely. Thus, the book might well be placed in a learning center at which students are to complete a task such as constructing a retrieval chart that shows each phrase of the Preamble, what it means in the student's own words, examples from the book, and examples that the student develops based on previous learning.

Poppy, written by Avi and illustrated by Brian Floca (New York: Orchard Books, 1995; intermediate, advanced), is the story of a family of deer mice who live under the rule of Mr. Ocax, a great horned owl. Mr. Ocax has declared himself king of the forest and the only being who can protect the deer mice from porcupines. When they disobey his rules, however, he eats them. Although young Poppy witnesses this horrible reprisal when Mr. Ocax eats her boyfriend, she volunteers to make the treacherous journey to a new farm house to which the family wants to move. On the way, she meets a wise porcupine, who clues her in to the fact that Mr. Ocax is afraid of porcupines and is, in fact, providing no protection to her family at all, simply using his rules as a way to control his own food supply. The story would be a good stimulant for discussion of where government gets its authority. What gave Mr. Ocax power over the deer mice? How did he maintain his power?

The government's role in managing disputes can be illustrated using nonfiction books about notable court decisions. One of a series on "Landmark Supreme Court Cases," *Brown v. Board of Education: Equal Schooling for All*, by Harvey Fireside and Sarah Betsy Fuller (Springfield, NJ: Enslow, 1994; advanced), describes the conflict over school desegregation, the arguments on both sides, the Court's decision, and the impact of the decision. Ten "Questions to Think About" conclude the book; each question could be assigned to a panel of students for discussion and research. Panels could make brief presentations to the class on their questions.

Vaclav Havel and the Velvet Revolution, by Jeffrey Symynkywicz (Parsippany, NJ: Dillon Press, 1995; intermediate), is a biography that can be used to illustrate how limited and unlimited government are different and how consent of the governed limits government in a democracy. Opening with the words "My people, your government has returned to you," the book traces Havel's efforts to bring change to the government of Czechoslovakia and the means that the Communist government used to suppress his ideas and restrict his freedoms.

Rules and Laws

Laws and rules are needed to guide behavior and establish order; laws and rules can be good or bad and can be changed.

Students, like adults, must deal with laws and rules every day and in every aspect of their lives. Thus, understanding the purposes of rules and laws and how rules and laws can be evaluated and changed are important aspects of citizenship. Rules and laws serve similar purposes but generally function in somewhat different settings. Rules, as well as customs, are used in families and in less complex settings while laws are enacted in complex societies. Both rules and laws may evolve from customs.

Laws and rules have multiple purposes, and these purposes may vary in different settings. Among the purposes for law in U.S. society are describing acceptable and unacceptable behavior; providing order, predictability, and security; protecting citizens' rights and providing benefits to citizens; assigning burdens or responsibilities; and limiting the power of people in authority. Of course, a single rule or law may address several of these purposes. For example, a law making burglary a crime describes acceptable/unacceptable behavior; provides for security; and protects citizens' property rights. As the purposes make clear, laws reflect the values of the society in which they are enacted.

While understanding laws and valuing the functions they serve in society is an important aspect of citizenship, students should also learn ways to evaluate rules and laws because not all rules and laws are good ones. According to the *National Standards for Civics and Government*, criteria for evaluating rules and laws include the following:

- Is the rule or law well designed to achieve its purpose?

- Is the rule or law understandable?

- Can people follow the rule or law?

- Is the rule or law fair to all people?

- Is the rule or law designed to protect individual rights and/or provide for the common good?

If a rule or law is a bad one, it should be changed. Thus, students should also learn how laws are changed and understand that individuals can work to change or maintain laws.

Better Not Get Wet, Jesse Bear, by Nancy White Carlstrom, illustrated by Bruce Degen (New York: Macmillan, 1988; primary), is a rhyming story of Jesse Bear, whose parents remind him not to get wet when he is drinking juice, washing dishes, watering plants, and taking part in a variety of activities. When it comes to playing in his own pool, however, getting wet is okay. The story can be used to stimulate discussion of the purposes of a rule like "Don't get wet," as well as the notion that rules may apply to particular situations or settings. Students could create a chart that shows rules they follow at home and at school, with columns showing when the rule applies and when it doesn't. For example, "No running" may apply in the school corridors and in the house at home, but not in the yard or on the playground.

Lilly's Purple Plastic Purse, by Kevin Henkes (New York: Greenwillow Books, 1996; primary), provides a good vehicle for discussing classroom rules and their purposes. Lilly loves school and especially her teacher, Mr. Slinger, but she also loves her new purple purse, which plays music when it is opened. When she disobeys Mr. Slinger and does not put her purse away, he confiscates her purse. This turn of events causes her to draw an insulting picture of the teacher, an action she later regrets. After reading the book, students could discuss both Mr. Slinger's and Lilly's actions. What classroom rule covered the situation involving Lilly's purse? What is the purpose of this rule? Why didn't Lilly obey it? What would happen to the class if everyone acted like Lilly did when she brought her new purse to class? Does that help us understand why we need rules? Was the punishment Lilly received fair? Why or why not?

Old Henry, by Joan W. Blos, illustrated by Stephen Gammell (New York: William Morrow, 1987; primary), is a rhyming story about a man who does not live by the same standards as his neighbors. He doesn't take care of his lawn or fix up the old house in which he lives. The angry neighbors write letters, ask the city to fine him, and threaten jail, but still Henry does not change. Even being nice does not work. Not until Henry moves away do the neighbors realize that he had other good qualities that added to their neighborhood. After reading this story, students could discuss why there might be a law requiring that people fix their houses and take care of their yards. What would be good about a law like that? What would be bad? In general, do students think we should have such laws? What could be done about people, like Henry, who do not follow the laws?

Arnie and the Stolen Markers, written and illustrated by Nancy Carlson (New York: Viking, 1987; primary), deals with laws that are probably quite familiar to students—laws against stealing. After spending all of his money on candy, Arnie sees a set of wonderful markers and slips them under his shirt as he runs out the door. When his mother finds the markers, he confesses, and she sends him back to Harvey's store to return the markers. Fearing jail, Arnie instead must work for a week in Harvey's store. After reading the story, students could discuss reasons for shoplifting laws and whether the punishment for Arnie's crime was a good one. What makes a punishment just?

Books about family and school rules can also have relevance to older students. *Junebug*, by Alice Mead (New York: HarperCollins, 1995; intermediate), is the gripping story of a nine-year-old boy who lives in low-income projects in New Haven, Connecticut. Junebug and his younger sister Tasha must obey what will likely seem to many students like an over-abundance of rules designed to protect their safety. As Junebug's aunt and friends begin to slide into a life that involves drugs and crime, he remains true to the values his mother has taught him—loyalty, responsibility, and learning. As he launches 50 messages in bottles on his tenth birthday, the reader cannot help admire his courage and perservance. Among the many topics that could be discussed in relationship to the book is why safety rules vary from place to place. What rules necessary for Junebug are not necessary in other neighborhoods? What safety rules might be necessary in a farm community that would seem strange to Junebug?

The first chapter of *Bad Girls*, by Cynthia Voight (New York: Scholastic, 1996; intermediate, advanced), presents a hilarious look at school rules in the classroom of a fifth-grade teacher known to be the strictest in the school, if not the entire town. Mrs. Chemsky has 17 firmly established rules (in such catagories as forbidding rules, behavior rules, and lunch rules). While the presentation is light-hearted, it could motivate students to consider the purposes of various kinds of classroom rules, perhaps as a precursor to developing rules for their own classroom.

Older students can look at conflicts around school rules via a book such as *Nothing But the Truth* (New York: Orchard Books, 1991; advanced), in which author Avi tells the story through such documents as ninth-grader Philip Malloy's diary, letters from his English teacher, Miss Narwin, to her sister, school memos, transcripts of phone calls, and newspaper clippings. Through these documents, the reader must put together the "truth" of what happens when Philip is suspended for humming during the playing of the national anthem as part of morning announcements. Philip's case becomes a First Amendment *cause celebre*, although his reasons for breaking the rule requiring standing at silent, respectful attention have little to do with freedom of expression and much to do with getting out of Miss Narwin's class. While reading the book, students might discuss the reasons for the rule, the political factors that influenced how the conflict is handled, and whether the punishment was appropriate. Whether what ultimately happens to both Philip and Miss Narwin is fair is a question that should provoke debate.

A book that presents a set of problems for which new laws or rules may be required provides another stimulant to student thinking about this theme. For example, the book *Everglades*, by Jean Craighead George, illustrated by Wendell Minor (New York: HarperCollins, 1995; primary, intermediate), paints a picture of the Everglades as it was before human settlement, followed by a description of how people changed and endangered the habitat and the animals living there. The storyteller suggests that the children listening to the story will be the ones to save the Everglades. After hearing or reading the book, students could work in groups to draft new laws that would help protect an ecosystem such as the Everglades. Other groups could then evaluate the proposed laws, using criteria like those described above.

For older students, Jean Craighead George's *There's an Owl in the Shower*, illustrated by Christine Herman Merrill (New York: HarperCollins, 1995; intermediate, advanced), could provide a stimulant for discussion of whether certain laws protecting the environment are a good idea or not. In this charming story, young Borden brings home a half-starved owlet, not realizing it is one of the hated spotted owls that cost his father his job as a lumberman. As the family grows to love the owl, they begin to realize the full complexity of issues involving the environment and the economy. While George's perspective is that of an environmentalist, she helps the reader understand the frustration of those whose livelihoods are threatened by environmental legislation. Thus, the book would provide an excellent impetus for discussing the costs and benefits of various kinds of laws.

Older students could explore the relationship between laws and values through reading and discussion of *The Giver*, by Lois Lowry (Boston: Houghton Mifflin, 1993; advanced). This Newbery-award-winning novel vividly creates a world in which children at age 12 are given the job assignments they will fulfill for life. Young Jonas, the hero of the story, is given a very special assignment, being the receiver of memories no longer available to the people in this society—memories of colors, of music and love, but also of pain and conflict. Jonas and his mentor, the Giver of the title, eventually decide on a plan that will restore memory to the community and thereby create the need for a new system of laws. One of the highest values of this society is sameness; others are predictability and order. In discussing the book, students could examine how the rules of the society support these values. They might then create their own rules for a society with other values; different groups could choose different values and compare their results to see how these differing values create different rules or laws. Teaching ideas related to this book can be found online at http://www.bdd.com/forum/bddforum.cgi/trc/index/give.

Democratic Values and Principles

Our democratic government is based on values and principles in which Americans believe.

According to the *National Standards for Civics and Government*, the "fundamental values and principles of American democracy provide common ground for Americans to work together to promote the attainment of individual, community, and national goals....These shared values and principles have helped to promote cohesion in the daily life of Americans and in times of crisis..."

The values and principles that underlie our democratic government are set forth in a variety of important documents, particularly the Declaration of Independence and the Constitution.

Students should understand the importance of shared values and recognize what some of those values are. Many different lists of fundamental democratic values have been created. For example, Lockwood and Harris (1985) suggest that, for curricular purposes, fundamental democratic values can be defined as follows:

- Authority: a value concerning what rules or people should be obeyed and the consequences for disobedience.

- Equality: a value concerning whether people should be treated in the same way.

- Liberty: a value concerning what freedoms people should have and the limits that may justifiably be placed on them.

- Life: a value concerning when, if ever, it is justifiable to threaten or take a life.

- Loyalty: a value concerning obligations to the people, traditions, ideas, and organizations of importance in one's life.

- Promise-keeping: a value concerning the nature of duties that arise when promises are made.

- Property: a value concerning what people should be allowed to own and how they should be allowed to use it.

- Truth: a value concerning the expression, distortion, or withholding of accurate information.

The *National Standards* suggest such values as individual rights to life, liberty, property, and the pursuit of happiness; the public or common good; justice; equality of opportunity; diversity; truth; and patriotism.

The standards also list fundamental principles of American democracy. These principles are:

- The people are sovereign.

- The power of government is limited by law.

- People exercise their authority directly and indirectly.

- Decisions are based on majority rule, but minority rights are protected.

Shared values are important, at least in part, because they form the foundation for a sense of community. While shared values are important, however, the United States has benefited from the diversity of its people's viewpoints. Students should therefore understand the benefits of diversity, as well as its costs and methods for managing or preventing conflicts about diversity.

Looking at holidays is one way for young students to learn about democratic values. Holidays both celebrate shared values and history and transmit those values to younger generations. A less familiar holiday celebrating freedom is chronicled in *Juneteenth Jamboree*, by Carole Boston Weatherford, illustrated by Yvonne Buchanan (New York: Lee and Low, 1995; primary). Young Cassie's family has recently moved to Texas. On June 19, her parents are cooking up a storm and keeping a secret from Cassie—the family is going to a jamboree to recognize the day on which slaves in Texas learned they were free—more than two years after the Emancipation Proclamation was issued. Storytellers, a parade, music, and fabulous food are all part of the celebration. At the end, each person releases a balloon with a strip of paper inside; on one side is written "Forever Free," on the other the person's name. Discuss with students why this is a suitable way to celebrate freedom. What other holidays celebrate freedom? What kinds of celebrations are traditional at these holidays? Encourage students to think of a new "tradition" for celebrating freedom.

Peter Spier presents a look at diversity as an American value in *People* (New York: Delacorte, 1980; primary, intermediate), a book illustrated in his typical style with scores of small and larger, but incredibly detailed illustrations. Spier illustrates the many ways in which people are diverse and concludes that life would be very dull if everyone were the same. Each page deserves in-depth examination and enjoyment. After reading the book, students could make a book about the diversity within their classroom, with a section on how each student's unique strengths make life in the class more interesting.

Two classic collections of poems edited by Myra Cohn Livingston—*Calooh! Callay!* (New York: Atheneum, 1978; intermediate, advanced) and *O Frabjous Day!* (New York: Atheneum 1977; intermediate, advanced)—can be used to help older students examine the links between holidays and shared democratic values. Another collection of poetry that can help older students recognize the importance of democratic values is *Hand in Hand: An American History Through Poetry*, collected by Lee Bennett Hopkins, illustrated by Peter M. Fiore (New York: Simon and Schuster, 1994; intermediate, advanced). Poems included range from classics, such as Longfellow's description of Paul Revere's ride and "The New Colossus," by Emma Lazarus, to less familiar works, such as a poem from a plaque dedicated to Harriet Tubman, a poem on the HUAC by Langston Hughes, and a work on homeless people by compiler Hopkins. In all of these collections, some poems celebrate our shared values, while others point out cases in which we have fallen short in living up to those values. Discussion of these poems can help students recognize that while our society does not always reflect achievement of our values, the values provide goals to strive for. After reading a number of poems, students could select several important democratic values and write and illustrate poems about those values to create a class anthology that could be shared with other students and parents.

Stories that illustrate how values are reflected in everyday life are another valuable approach to this "big idea." For example, *Mayfield Crossing*, by Vaunda Micheaux Nelson, illustrated by Leonard Jenkins (New York: Putnam's, 1993; intermediate; advanced), illustrates why the values of tolerance and equality of opportunity are necessary for a community—including a community of youngsters—to function in a way that works for everyone. When their school closes, the children of Mayfield Crossing must go to a larger school where their new classmates treat them poorly—some simply because the Mayfield children are new, others because a few of the Mayfield children are African American. As the Mayfield Crossing children work hard to do well and try to make new friends, they also learn to be more tolerant of an eccentric veteran who lives in their neighborhood.

In the Year of the Boar and Jackie Robinson, by Betto Bao Lord (New York: Harper and Row, 1984; intermediate, advanced), is based on the author's own experiences as a young immigrant in New York City. The main character, Shirley Temple Wong, learns to love baseball and, specifically, the Brooklyn Dodgers, a love that provides a bond with her new classmates. Their teacher uses their love of baseball to give them a civics lesson, showing how baseball and American democracy share many values, such as equal opportunity, teamwork, and the ability to change things for the better. The same chapter of the book includes Shirley's hilarious rendition of the Pledge of Allegiance, which her emerging English skills have not yet made sense of. This version could be used to prompt analysis of the Pledge of Allegiance and the values included in it. Older students could create analogies between democracy and other sports or games as a way of demonstrating their under-standing of democratic values.

The Well, by Mildred D. Taylor (New York: Dial Books, 1995; advanced), is a short novel that recounts the events in the lives of two African-American boys in the South in the early 1900s. The two brothers, David and Hammer Logan, are happy to share their family's water during the summer drought—with everyone except the bigoted and mean Simms family. Tensions between the Logan and Simms boys mount through a series of encounters, with the local sheriff siding with the white Simms family. When the Simms boys throw a skunk and other dead animals into the Logan family's well, even their father realizes they have gone too far. The story beautifully presents both positive and negative values but would be especially valuable as a stimulant to discussing injustice.

Crash, a funny yet touching novel by Jerry Spinelli (New York: Knopf, 1996; advanced), provides a springboard for discussing a number of democratic values and how they are evident in our everyday lives. Crash, A.K.A. John Coogan, is a seventh-grader whose physi-cal size allows him to exercise power—without authority—over classmates. Crash thinks both his sister Abby and his neighbor, Penn Webb, are dweebs, especially when they get involved in protesting a new shopping mall. As a series of adventures take Crash and his family (including grandfather Scooter, a key character) and friends through the school year, however, he begins to respect values that Penn and Abby practice—honesty, caring, hard work, and nonviolence. When he gives up his chance to run in the Penn Relays (for which Penn himself was named), Crash has become a new man. In the story, Penn wears buttons and T-shirts that his mother makes and that express his values (e.g., Peace and Hug a Tree). As a follow-up activity, students could design buttons, T-shirts, or bumper stickers that promote values they think are important to our democracy. Students could also write the next chapter of the book—what do they think will happen to Crash in eighth-grade? Will he continue to be a football star? Will he run in the Penn Relays? Might he get involved in environmental causes, like Abby and Penn? Will he and Jane Forbes strike up a friend-ship—or more?

Tonight, by Sea, by Frances Temple (New York: Orchard Books, 1995; advanced), allows students to examine the relationship between democracy and fundamental values by looking at a country where achieving democracy has been difficult—Haiti. Set in Haiti in 1993, the book tells of a small community building a boat in hopes of escaping to the United States. Children and adults talk about the exiled leader Aristide, whose ideas for a democracy in Haiti were based on the value of social justice. Under the dictatorship ruling the island nation, however, even life is not valued. The book should spark discussion of the differences between democracies and dictatorships, as well as how the United States can help promote democratic values in other countries.

Music from a Place Called Half Moon, by Jerrie Oughton (Boston: Houghton Mifflin, 1995; advanced), is a moving story that illustrates some of the costs and benefits of diversity at a very personal level. Set in a small town in North Carolina, the story illustrates how the behavior of members of different ethnic groups affects others in negative ways. The central character is eighth-grader Edie Jo, who feels torn apart by her experiences. Her father argues for integrating vacation Bible school and her family is shunned by other whites in town; she and her brother are harassed by four young Native American men; when her grandmother insults two Native Americans, her house is burned down. Edie concludes that she hates all groups that are different from her—until she becomes friends with Cherokee Fish, whose love of music, dreams of changing his life, and respect for Edie's own talents show her that the color of a person's skin does not determine his/her value.

Two books could provide interesting models for sharing what students have learned about important democratic values. *A Children's Chorus* (New York: Dutton, 1988; all levels) presents the principles on which the United Nations Declaration of the Rights of the Child (1959) were based. Each principle is illustrated by a different award-winning illustrator; the illustrations are both visually appealing and thought-provoking. Students could read the principles and discuss what each means. Students could then select democratic principles or values that they believe are important and create a similar illustrated book explaining what those principles or values mean in everyday life. The book could be shared with younger students in the school.

William Bennett's *The Book of Virtues for Young People* (Parsippany, NJ: Silver Burdett, 1996; advanced) is a collection of stories, fables, and poems organized around "virtues," some of which parallel the democratic values listed above. Students could examine the pieces that Bennett has selected to illustrate a virtue/value such as "loyalty." They could then develop a list of democratic values they wish to illustrate and collect stories, drawings, and so on to illustrate each. Again, the collections could be shared with other classes in the school.

Citizens' Rights and Privileges

Citizens have rights and privileges that are protected by the Constitution.

The meaning of citizenship is clearly a key understanding for all young people. Citizenship is legal recognition of a person's membership in a nation; citizens have legally protected rights and privileges.

In the United States, citizens have a wide range of rights that are protected by the government. According to the *National Standards*, these include:

- Personal rights, such as the right to associate, practice one's religious beliefs, travel freely, and so on.

- Political rights, such as the right to vote, speak freely, join a political party, hold public office, have a fair trial if accused of a crime, and so on.

- Economic rights, such as the right to own property, to establish a business, and to join a labor union, and so on.

Many rights are protected by the Constitution, specifically by the Bill of Rights, while others are protected by laws enacted by Congress. Rights are not absolute, however. When rights conflict with other important rights or values, controversy may arise regarding what limits should be placed on rights.

Literature can be used in at least two ways to develop this understanding. The first method of using books would be to select books that focus on the importance of particular rights to people, either in the United States or in other countries. The second method would be to use books that have as their dramatic core the conflict between rights and other important values.

As an example of the first use, consider the right to vote. Perhaps no right is so often taken for granted. Many works of children's literature provide a means for reminding students that the right is one that many people have had to fight very hard to obtain and have gone to great lengths to exercise when it finally became available to them. For example, *The Day Gogo Went to Vote*, by Elinor Batezat Sisulu, illustrated by Sharon Wilson (Boston: Little, Brown, 1996; primary, intermediate), tells the story of an elderly South African woman who wants to vote in the 1994 elections, the first open to black South Africans. As she, her family, and election officials make special efforts to make that happen, her young granddaughter learns not only about the process of elections but about the importance of voting.

Books on the women's suffrage movement, which have been written for students at all levels, can also be used to highlight the importance of the right to vote. *The Ballot Box Battle*, by Emily Arnold McCully (New York: Knopf, 1996; primary), tells parallel stories of a young girl's struggle for acceptance and her neighbor's efforts to vote (her neighbor just happens to be Elizabeth Cady Stanton). The story's message is that voting is a way of asserting a person's value and that voting is a right worth fighting for. A similar theme is developed in *A Long Way to Go*, by Zibby O'Neal, illustrated by Michael Dooling (New York: Puffin Books, 1990; intermediate). Young Lila must struggle with her parents' and brothers' restricted views of what girls can do while learning about her grandmother's efforts on behalf of women's suffrage. Elizabeth Cady Stanton's story is told in Jean Fritz's lively biographical style in *You Want Women to Vote, Lizzie Stanton?*, illustrated by DyAnne DiSalvo-Ryan (New York: Putnam's, 1995; intermediate, advanced). Susan B. Anthony is a major character in *Radical Red*, by James Duffy (New York: Simon and Schuster, 1993; advanced), which tells how a young girl and her mother become involved in the suffrage movement, despite the opposition of their father/husband. Scales (1996) annotates additional books on this topic and provides teaching suggestions.

Another way of using literature to help students understand the importance of citizens' rights is to use books about immigrants, many of whom come to the United States because they do not have rights in their home countries. Children's books on the theme of immigration are numerous, and many deal with rights in ways that will be new to students. For example, *Dancing to America*, by Ann Morris, photographs by Paul Kolnik (New York: Dutton, 1994; intermediate, advanced), tells the story of young Anton Pankevich, whose family emigrated from the Soviet Union to gain both religious freedom and greater freedom of expression (through dance) for Anton. As with the topic of suffrage, books on immigration are available at all grade levels. For example, *In America*, written and illustrated by Marissa Moss (New York: Dutton, 1994: primary), tells a grandfather's story of coming to America from Lithuania to gain religious freedom. *Letters from Rifka*, by Karen Hesse (New York: Henry Holt, 1992; intermediate; advanced), is also a story of immigration to gain religious (and other) freedoms. Told in the form of letters written by 12-year-old Rifka to her cousin who remained in Russia, the book highlights the difficulties immigrants of all ages faced in their search for freedom. By focusing on the reasons that people could be excluded from the United States, it also provides a stimulant to discussion of whether rights are—and should be—available to everyone who comes here.

Raintree/Steck-Vaughan publishes a series of books entitled "Why We Left." Each book provides a historic and geographic overview of the subject country, narrated by an elementary-age child. The text also includes a discussion of why the narrator's family left their home country. For example, the family of the narrator in *I Remember China*, by Anita Ganeri (Austin, TX: Raintree/Steck-Vaughan, 1995; primary, intermediate), supported the students protesting for more democratic government in Tiananmen Square in 1989; because of their beliefs, they no longer felt safe in China, thus illustrating the importance of freedom of conscience and expression. Other countries or areas covered in the series include Somalia, India, Palestine, Bosnia, and Vietnam.

A focus only on people coming to the United States because they were deprived of rights in another country might lead students to conclude that Americans' rights have never been taken away. To counter this notion, books on a topic such as the Japanese-American internment during World War II could be used to foster discussion of what happens to Americans and to American democracy when U.S. citizens are deprived of their rights. Again, this is a topic on which books have been written for students of diverse ages and reading levels; a few examples are described here.

The Bracelet, by Yoshiko Uchida, illustrated by Joanna Yardley (New York: Philomel Books, 1993; primary), tells the story of a little girl who receives a bracelet from her best friend on the day she leaves her home. Although she vows never to take it off, in the first frightening day at a racetrack turned into an internment camp, Emi somehow loses the bracelet. Emi's mother helps her realize that she can remember her friend without the bracelet, just as they can remember their father, who has been sent to a prisoner of war camp in Montana. Although the book does not belabor what has happened to Emi's family, it does make clear how frightening and disorienting the loss of one's everyday life was.

Baseball Saved Us, by Ken Mochizuki, illustrated by Dom Lee (New York: Lee and Low Books, 1993; primary, intermediate), tells the story of "Shorty" and his family, who are among the thousands of Japanese Americans forcibly relocated by the government. Fighting physical and psychological hardships, they turn to baseball as a way not only to pass the time but to gain dignity and self-respect.

"In Response to Executive Order 9066," by Dwight Okita, is a moving poem available in the collection *Celebrate America in Poetry and Art*, edited by Nora Panzer (New York: Hyperion Books, 1994; all ages). In just one page, it tells about a Japanese-American child's loss of her best friend because of the relocation order. Confused and hurt, the child hopes her friend will miss her when she is gone.

The Invisible Thread, by Yoshiko Uchida (New York: Julian Messner, 1991; intermediate, advanced), is a memoir in which Uchida recounts her childhood in northern California, her father's imprisonment after Pearl Harbor, and the family's internment at the Topaz camp in Utah. The effects of prejudice and the internment itself are well portrayed, as are the family's life and very American dreams prior to the war. Students could compare this memoir with the fictional accounts Uchida produced in *Journey to Topaz* (New York: Scribner's, 1971) and *Journey Home* (New York: Atheneum, 1978), which draw upon Uchida's experiences but also add a character who served in the 442nd and must deal with guilt and grief over a friend's death.

A Fence Away from Freedom: Japanese Americans and World War II, by Ellen Levine (New York: Putnam's, 1995; intermediate, advanced), is a collection of oral histories from Japanese Americans who were children or young adults at the time of World War II. Life before the war, the immediate effects of Pearl Harbor, and life in the camps are covered, as are less familiar topics that are equally important: internment of Japanese-American orphans, Japanese Peruvians who were brought to U.S. camps to be exchanged for U.S. prisoners in Japan, resisters and those who renunciated their U.S. citizenship, life outside camp, and the effects of the movement for reparations. Older students who read this book could be organized into groups, with each group taking responsibility for one chapter, designing a museum display that would educate others about what they learned in their chapter, focusing particularly on the loss of rights, how that loss affected people, and actions taken to protest the goverment's actions or to regain rights in other ways.

Books focusing on a particular right are also useful in developing understanding of this "big idea." For example, Patricia Polacco's charming *Aunt Chip and the Great Triple Creek Dam Affair* (New York: Philomel Books, 1996; primary, intermediate) highlights what happens when a city sacrifices its right to read books. Aunt Chip was the librarian in Triple Creek when the town fathers decided to close the library and started using books to repair potholes, slumping buildings, and a leaking dam. Aunt Chip took to her bed for 50 years but reemerges when young Eli and his friends show interest in reading. The result is both comical and an affirmation of the importance of free expression and a free press.

Conflicts among rights or between rights and values are also common in children's literature. *The Conversation Club*, written and illustrated by Diane Stanley (New York: Macmillan, 1983; primary, intermediate), provides an example of such a conflict that even the youngest children can understand. Peter Fieldmouse, who has just moved into the neighborhood, is invited to join the neighbors' conversation club. Each member has a specialty—from cooking to sports to ghost stories. Peter is horrified, however, when he discovers that they all exercise their freedom of speech at once. Peter stomps out of the meeting, declaring that he will start his own club, which will be devoted to listening. When the neighbors join this club, whose initial rule that no one can speak is eventually changed to one person speaks at a time, they recognize that placing limits on themselves can actually improve their community. The book might be introduced by having students all talk at once while the teacher gives directions that would lead to a privilege or treat—if students could hear them. The students' discovery that everyone talking at the same time caused them to miss an opportunity could be used as a stimulus to discussing whether they would limit their freedom of speech in order to make sure they do not miss opportunities. The class could then read the book, stopping at various points to discuss ways in which the problems that arise could be resolved.

Richard Peck's *The Last Safe Place on Earth* (New York: Delacorte, 1995; advanced) provides an example in which the right to free expression conflicts with a variety of other rights and values. Members of a church protest books that are read in the local junior high, claiming that the books violate their religious beliefs. The parents of a young girl frightened by the stories of a babysitter who belongs to the church believe that the young woman has violated their trust. A student reporter on the school paper is frustrated by the editor's refusal to carry stories on topics she believes are important; when she takes her stories to the town newspaper, however, the editor of the school paper is angry. All of these characters and situations (and others) make for a gripping and thought-provoking story that should provoke discussion of what happens when rights conflict. Two interesting questions to consider would be: What is the author's position on the rights that are in conflict in this story? How might the story be different if it had been written by someone with a different point of view? For example, what if the story were written from Laurel's point of view instead of Todd's?

Gary Paulsen's *The Rifle* (San Diego: Harcourt Brace, 1995; advanced) is a disturbing story highlighting the conflict between the right to bear arms and the right to life. Paulsen first details the creation of a "sweet" rifle—a weapon of uncommon beauty and accuracy— and its use in the Revolutionary War. Rediscovered in an attic in 1993, the rifle ends up above the mantel of a service station operator's home. Paulsen then recounts the childhood of a young man named Richard. Ultimately, the rifle and Richard cross paths when a fireplace spark ignites the powder still in the rifle and Richard is killed. Again, students should consider the author's viewpoint. Which of the conflicting rights does Paulsen value more?

What is his purpose in writing the book? Has he achieved that purpose? How would the book be different if written from a different perspective?

Of course, nonfiction works on conflicts among rights are also available. Doreen Rappaport takes an especially interesting approach in her book, *Tinker vs. Des Moines: Student Rights on Trial* (New York: HarperCollins, 1993; advanced). The book includes narrative text about the famous free speech case, as well as newspaper clippings, excerpts from the trial transcripts and the judge's decisions, and interviews with major "players" in the case 27 years later. Throughout the text, the author provides questions to help students clarify their thinking about the case. The presentation is much more exciting than a typical nonfiction book on a landmark Supreme Court case and could easily be used to structure a mock trial or moot court simulation activity. The book is one in a series entitled "Be the Judge, Be the Jury."

Participation in Civic Life

Good citizens participate in civic life to promote the common good and to protect and improve our American democracy.

Too often, young people (and adults) think of obeying the law, voting, and holding public office (and perhaps jury duty) as the primary activities of citizens. These activities are certainly important ways of acting as a responsible citizen, and students should have opportunities to consider what characteristics they should look for in someone running for public office, how they can stay informed about candidates and ballot issues, and how they themselves can take a leadership role. Students should also be aware of such other ways that citizens take part in political life, such as paying taxes and serving in the armed forces.

Books that deal with these basic citizen responsibilities are available. For example, *Believing Sophie*, by Hazel Hutchins, illustrated by Dorothy Donohue (Morton Grove, IL: Albert Whitman, 1995; primary), is the story of a little girl who is falsely accused of shoplifting. The fear and hurt she experiences until she is able to prove her innocence are well portrayed in both the text and drawings. Students could discuss why, when a person believes in obeying the law, he or she would feel so bad about being accused of breaking it.

Peacebound Trains, by Haemi Balgassi, illustrated by Chris K. Soentpeet (New York: Clarion, 1996; primary, intermediate), presents two generations' stories of sacrifice to serve in their country's armed forces. Sumi is a Korean-American child who misses her mother, away from home in the army. Her grandmother shares a story with her of many years ago in Korea, when her husband sent his family to safety on a train but stayed behind to fight the communists. The sacrifices made by citizens serving in the military are depicted in a way that is understandable and should prompt discussion among students.

However, the activities of the good citizen go far beyond these activities. Good citizens try to influence their government in a variety of ways—by communicating with public officials, voting, taking a role in interest groups, attending meetings of government agencies, working in campaigns, circulating and signing petitions, taking part in demonstrations, and so on. In order to be effective, good citizens inform themselves about public issues, monitor the actions of governments at all levels, and develop the skills needed to communicate their positions.

Good citizens also take part in civic life in other ways, ways that do not necessarily relate directly to government but do promote the common good and improve our democracy. These activities of good citizens include taking the opportunity to be educated, working to support their families, volunteering in the community, treating all people with respect, and the like. These kinds of actions are critical in building community, a belief that one shares goals with one's neighbors (defined broadly) and will work together to achieve those goals and to solve common problems.

Certain dispositions or character traits enhance the likelihood that a person will be a good citizen. According to the *National Standards for Civics and Government*, these dispositions include the following: individual responsibility, self-discipline/self-governance, civility, respect for the rights of other individuals, honesty, respect for the law, open mindedness, critical mindedness, negotiation and compromise, persistence, civic mindedness, compassion, and patriotism. A person with these traits is more likely to practice civic virtue—that is, to put the common good above one's own personal interests.

Literature provides many models of these dispositions, as well as of people who are (and are not) good citizens. Such models can be found in both fiction and nonfiction, particularly biographies. As students read books featuring characters who show their civic virtue in a variety of ways, they might make a "Citizens Hall of Fame," featuring posters that show what aspects of good citizenship each character represents. Older students could look for news stories about real people who manifest the same characteristics as the fictional characters. Some fictional works that provide useful models of citizenship include the following:

Jamaica Louise James, by Amy Hest, illustrated by Sheila White Samton (Cambridge, MA: Candlewick Press, 1996; primary), is the story of young girl who loves to draw. When she decides to create a series of paintings to enliven the subway station where her grandmother works, the unintended consequence is a place where everyone becomes friendlier and happier. The mayor ends up putting Jamaica's name on a plaque in the subway station. After reading the book, students might discuss areas in your community that could benefit from beautification efforts, brainstorm ways to make these areas more visually appealing, and find out how beautification efforts could be undertaken.

Peter's Place, by Sally Grindley, illustrated by Michael Foreman (New York: Gulliver, 1995; primary), describes a special place on the beach where young Peter loves to play and feed the animals. When an oil tanker breaks apart on the rocks nearby, Peter and others must work nonstop for days to save the wildlife. While most students are not likely to be faced with a similar challenge, *Peter's Place* could be followed by a book presenting a more common environmental problem, such as *Where Once There Was a Wood*, by Denise Fleming (New York: Henry Holt, 1996; primary). Fleming, in brilliantly colored illustrations and simple text, depicts the loss of wildlife habitat to human homes and then describes how backyards, schoolyards, and other urban spaces can be used to create habitats for wildlife, a project that could be undertaken by students at home or school.

Uncle Willie and the Soup Kitchen, written and illustrated by DyAnne DiSalvo-Ryan (New York: Morrow, 1991; primary, intermediate), tells the story of a young boy who is frightened by homeless people in his neighborhood. When he helps his Uncle Willie work at the soup kitchen one day, he gains a new perspective on the problems of people who are hungry, as well as new respect for his uncle and the others who work at the soup kitchen. After reading the book, students could talk about what characteristics and actions make Uncle Willie a good citizen. They could also discuss why, near the end of the book, the author uses the word *citizens* to describe the people who eat at the soup kitchen. Why did she pick this word? What is she trying to remind readers of? Students could also follow up by researching whether your community has a soup kitchen and how they might help the agency do its work. They could also talk to volunteers at the soup kitchen to find out why they volunteer their time for such a cause.

Come Back, Salmon: How a Group of Dedicated Kids Adopted Pigeon Creek and Brought It Back to Life, by Molly Cone, photographs by Sidnee Wheelwright (San Francisco: Sierra Club Books, 1992; intermediate), is a detailed account of not only how students saved the creek but what they learned while doing it and the rewards they realized. The book could be used to kick off an integrated unit on waterways and citizens' role in protecting them.

Junebug (see annotation on page 11) provides a moving model of the character traits that enhance the likelihood that a person will be a good citizen. Through trying times, the title character shows responsiblity, self-discipline, civility, respect for the law, compassion, and persistence beyond his years. He also has hope for the future, certainly a key to working for an improved democracy. Students who read this book might want to plan their own launching of bottles with messages in them, as Junebug did on his birthday.

The 1997 Newbery-winner is a delightful book about how a group of sixth-graders and their teacher create a community based on caring, civility, kindness, and learning. *The View from Saturday,* by E.L. Konigsburg (New York: Atheneum, 1996; intermediate, advanced), tells the story of an Academic Bowl team's triumphs, interspersed with chapters narrated by each of its members; these chapters, which could be self-contained short stories, provide insight into the experiences that led these four youngsters to create a small community around their paraplegic teacher. This would be a good book to read early in the year as a basis for discussing the values on which classroom interactions in your class will be based.

Until Whatever, by Martha Humphries (New York: Clarion, 1991; advanced), tells what happens when cheerleader Karen decides not to follow the crowd and renews a friendship with Annie, a student with AIDS. When Karen's long-time friends turn their backs on her, she turns to the press to make a plea for tolerance. The courage Karen and Annie must demonstrate in this rough school year should prompt student discussion of the possible costs of doing the right thing. After reading and discussing the book, students could write newspaper articles on the need for tolerance in their own community.

For older students, many nonfiction books tell how ordinary and extraordinary people have worked to promote the common welfare. The content of Phillip Hoose's *It's Our World, Too* (Boston: Little, Brown, 1993; advanced) is well explained by its subtitle—*Young People Who Are Making a Difference.* Hoose provides a brief history of young people's efforts to improve the United States, followed by profile of 13 individuals and three groups that are currently working for causes larger than themselves. The book concludes with a handbook of strategies for working for change, strategies students who read the book may wish to implement in your community.

Milton Meltzer's *Who Cares? Millions Do...A Book About Altruism* (New York: Walker, 1994; advanced) looks primarily at larger organizational efforts, such as Habitat for Humanity, Amnesty International, and Volunteers of America, but also stresses how ordinary people can become involved in and even start such an organization. Anne Schraff looks at truly extraordinary people's efforts to promote the common welfare in *Women of Peace: Nobel Peace Prize Winners* (Springfield, NJ: Enslow, 1994; advanced). She provides brief biographies of Baroness von Suttner, Jane Addams, Emily Greene Balch, Mairead Corrigan and Betty Williams, Mother Teresa, Alva Myrdal, Daw Aung San Suu Kyi, and Rigoberta Menchu.

Individual students or small groups could read particular chapters of the above books and then share what they have learned with other students. For example, the class as a whole could create a "Civic Virtue" award. Students who have read about a particular person or group could then work together to write a speech nominating the person or group for the class award. Students could then present the speeches, and the class could vote on who should receive the award. Another option would be to create a talking timeline about the issue on which their activists worked. Each student could write a one-minute speech on the person or group, focusing on the problems addressed and what was accomplished. Students could then arrange themselves in chronological order and present their speeches, creating a talking timeline. This strategy would work particularly well for students who read *Women of Peace*. Students could also create visuals, such as mobiles, posters, or collages, that highlight the qualities that made the people they read about successful activists.

An interesting literary model of citizen action is *On the Wings of Peace* (New York: Clarion, 1995; advanced), to which a number of writers and artists have donated their work to advance a cause in which they believe, both by teaching young readers about peace and by raising money (through book sales) for organizations working for peace. Older students could use this model to prepare a book of their writing and art in support of some aspect of the common welfare.

References

Lockwood, Alan L., and David E. Harris, *Reasoning with Democratic Values: Instructor's Manual* (New York: Teachers College Press, 1985).

National Standards for Civics and Government (Calabasas: CA: Center for Civic Education, 1994).

Scales, Pat, "Jean Fritz's *You Want Women to Vote, Lizzie Stanton?*," *Book Links* (July 1996), pp. 47-51.

MODEL GUIDES FOR USING CHILDREN'S LITERATURE TO DEVELOP CIVIC UNDERSTANDINGS

Characteristics of a Good Guide

Susan Hepler has identified several characteristics for quality guides for literature-based programs. First, she says that "A good guide should improve the quality of the reader's experience with the book....Through talk, readers should be able to say, 'I hadn't thought about that before,' or 'I had, but I couldn't put it into words.'" A good guide should also include questions that cause students to "examine why people act as they do" and, in moderation, "encourage readers to identify with whatever aspects of the text match their perceptions." Finally, a good guide should include activities that "serve the reader and the book first, not some particular curriculum area."

In developing the guides included here, we have attempted to apply these criteria. Thus, although we emphasize civic understanding, we do not focus exclusively on citizenship. For each book, we include at least some questions that, like those used in the Great Books program, have "no single right answers, requiring both the student and teacher to examine factual information, assess motivation, and make inferences" (Gallagher 1991).

Each guide begins with a brief **Summary** of the book. This summary is followed by **Initiating Activities**, activities to be conducted prior to reading the book. Next we provide **Discussion Questions**. For longer books, these questions are divided into sections corresponding to sections of the book. The discussion questions are provided only as starters, not as a comprehensive list of the ideas or topics that should be discussed. Interesting issues are likely to emerge from students as they read and discuss the books. Each guide concludes with **Follow-up Activities**, which include a variety of instructional strategies for extending thinking and learning about ideas presented in the book.

Many of the books will be most effective if read aloud, especially with younger students. Having several copies of the book may still be a good idea, however, to allow close examination of the illustrations. For primary grade students, we include a relatively small number of questions in each guide. For older students, the number of questions increases, and we divide the list of questions by chapter or section of the book.

The chart on the next page lists the books for which guides are provided, appropriate grade levels, and civic understandings addressed.

References

Gallagher, Arlene F., ed., *Acting Together: Excerpts from Children's Literature on Themes from the Constitution* (Boulder, CO: Social Science Education Consortium, 1991).

Hepler, Susan, "A Guide for the Teacher Guides: Doing It Yourself," *The New Advocate* (Summer 1988).

Title	Grade Level	Govern-ment	Rules and Laws	Values and Principles	Rights and Privileges	Civic Participation
Roses Are Pink (32 pp.)	K-1		X	X		
Pearl Moscowitz's Last Stand (32 pp.)	K-2	X		X	X	X
Arthur Meets the President (32 pp.)	K-2	X		X		X
City Green (32 pp.)	K-2	X			X	X
A Very Important Day (32 pp.)	1-3				X	X
Granddaddy's Gift (32 pp.)	2-4		X	X	X	X
The Christmas Menorahs (39 pp.)	2-4	X		X	X	X
Mandela (38 pp.)	2-4		X	X	X	X
Eagle Song (80 pp.)	3-5	X		X		X
Brooklyn Doesn't Rhyme (86 pp.)	3-5			X	X	X
Stink Bomb Mom (154 pp.)	3-5		X		X	X
Off and Running (136 pp.)	3-5	X		X		X
The Great Squirrel Uprising (113 pp.)	3-5	X		X	X	X
Seedfolks (69 pp.)	3-5	X		X		X
Germy in Charge (150 pp.)	4-6	X		X		X
Marian Wright Edelman (128 pp.)	4-6	X	X	X	X	X
A Small Civil War (182 pp.)	5-6	X		X	X	X
Zlata's Diary (200 pp.)	5-6	X		X	X	X
Rio Grande Stories (257 pp.)	6+			X		X
The Bomb (195 pp.)	6+	X		X	X	X

Roses Are Pink, Your Feet Really Stink,
written and illustrated by Diane deGroat
(New York: Morrow Junior Books, 1996).

Summary

Because he thinks Margaret and Lewis have been mean to him, Gilbert writes a mean poem on each one's Valentine and then signs the other's name. After the teacher punishes the whole class for what appears to be Margaret and Lewis's misdeeds, the two put their heads together and figure out that Gilbert is responsible. When no one will play with Gilbert at recess, he regrets his actions and he and his friends are able to resolve their problem. Charmingly written and illustrated, the story demonstrates why it is important to "do the right thing."

Initiating Activities

1. Ask students if they can think of any special rules in your classroom that apply to special days or special activities. If they have difficulty, suggest rules that apply on holidays, during school assemblies, while using art or science supplies, for recess periods when the weather does not permit students to go outside, and so on. Ask why there are special rules for these kinds of days. Depending on the situation, the purposes may be to protect students against danger, to maintain order so other students can learn, to keep the room neat, to keep people's feelings from being hurt, and so on.

2. Show students the book and ask them to guess what special day the book is about. Generate some ideas for rules that might apply only to Valentine's Day. For each rule suggested, discuss what the purpose for that rule would be. Explain to students that the book is about someone who broke a special Valentine's Day rule and what happened because he did.

Discussion Questions

1. Why do you think Mrs. Byrd made a rule that students should write something nice to each of their classmates on Valentine's Day? Do you think this is a good Valentine's Day rule? Why or why not?

2. Why didn't Gilbert want to write nice valentine poems for Lewis and Margaret? Do you think Gilbert knew he was doing the wrong thing when he wrote mean valentines to Lewis and Margaret? What clue helped you decide on your answer?

3. How did getting nice valentines make Gilbert feel? How did getting mean valentines make Lewis and Margaret feel? Do their feelings help you understand the reasons for Mrs. Byrd's special rules?

4. What did Mrs. Byrd do after Lewis and Margaret stuck out their tongues at each other? Was this a fair punishment? Why or why not?

5. What happened when the other students found out that Gilbert wrote the mean valentines? How did Gilbert feel then?

6. Describe how Gilbert's problem was finally solved. What do you think Gilbert learned from this experience?

Follow-up Activities

1. Have students create "greeting cards" that contain poems about class rules that they think are important. The greeting cards could be saved and passed along to next year's students.

2. Organize the students into groups of four, with students playing Patty, Gilbert, Margaret, and Lewis. The students should role play ways that Gilbert could have let Margaret and Lewis know that they had made him unhappy without hurting their feelings. The groups can present their role plays to the class and the class can vote on the best solution.

Pearl Moscowitz's Last Stand,
by Arthur A. Levine, illustrated by Robert Roth
(New York: Tambourine Books, 1993).

Summary

Pearl Moscowitz lives on Gingko Street, a street that has changed in many ways in the years she has lived there. She has enjoyed watching the gingko trees planted when she was young grow tall and blossom, just as she has enjoyed getting acquainted with the people of various ethnic groups who have come to live on the street. When a man from the electric company comes to cut down the last gingko tree, she uses every strategy she can think of to save the tree. Finally, the mayor intervenes and saves the tree.

Initiating Activities

1. Ask students what we mean when we refer to someone's "last stand." Help them understand that a *stand* is a defense of something—sticking up for or fighting for it. When we say that something is a "last stand," it means they are defending something after a long fight or a series of fights.

2. Show students the cover illustration of the book and encourage them to study it in detail. Which person shown on the cover is Pearl Moscowitz? Who is the other person? Can you guess what he might be doing? What in the picture might Pearl be fighting for?

Discussion Questions

1. How did Bella Moscowitz, Pearl's mother, get trees planted on their street? Is this a good way to get action? Why or why not?

2. Describe some of the changes that took place in the years Pearl lived on Gingko Street. How did having many different kinds of people on Gingko Street make life there more interesting and fun?

3. What did the tall, thin man with thin lips and a thin tie want to do? Why? Why didn't Pearl want him to cut down the tree? What ways did Pearl use to try to stop him the first two days he came to Gingko Street? Do you think these methods would really work? Why or why not?

4. How would you solve the conflict between Pearl and the young man? What would you do if you were Pearl? The young man? The city government?

5. What was Pearl Moscowitz's last stand? How did the reporters help Pearl? Pretend that you are a TV reporter who interviewed Pearl while she was chained to the tree. What would you tell people about Pearl? What actions would you urge the public or the government to take?

6. How was the conflict resolved? Do you think this was a good way to resolve the conflict? Do you think Pearl got the "justice" she wanted? Explain your answer.

Follow-up Activities

1. Have students make a chart of the actions that the government (mayor) took in this story and the reasons for each action. Do students think these are good actions for a government official to take? Why or why not?

2. Ask students to consider what in their neighborhood they might make a "last stand" to defend. How would they make their last stand? Have students write and present puppet shows dramatizing last stands they believe would be worthwhile and effective.

3. Invite several senior citizens who live in the school neighborhood to visit your class and talk with students about changes they have observed in their neighborhood. Have they opposed any changes? If so, what were their reasons and what methods did they use?

> # *Arthur Meets the President*,
> ## written and illustrated by Marc Brown
> ## (Boston: Little, Brown, 1991).

Summary

In this title in the popular series about Arthur and his friends, Arthur enters and wins an essay contest on "How I Can Help Make America Great." The prize is a trip to Washington, DC, for Arthur's entire class, as well as the chance to read his essay in front of the president. Arthur is so nervous he can barely speak, but the antics of his sister, D.W., save the day.

Initiating Activities

1. Ask whether students are familiar with the character Arthur and encourage them to share what they know about the character, his family, and friends.

2. Read the title of the book to students and ask them to speculate on why Arthur might meet the president. What are some of the reasons that ordinary citizens meet the president? Share with students some newspaper stories or articles you have collected about ordinary citizens receiving awards or recognition from the president.

Discussion Questions

1. What contest did Arthur and his classmates enter? Based on what Arthur was thinking, what do you think he wrote about? What would you write about for such a contest?

2. Why do you think the president would sponsor such a contest? Do you think encouraging people to help make America great is part of the president's job? Why or why not?

3. What do teachers mean when they say "do your best work"? Do you like contests in which you must do your best work? Why or why not?

4. How did everyone at school feel when Arthur won the contest? How did Arthur feel? What was making him nervous? What would you suggest to make him less nervous?

5. What were some of the famous sites that Arthur and his class saw in Washington, DC? Why do you think people go to visit these sites?

6. Describe what happened when the president arrived and when Arthur gave his speech. What did you think was the funniest thing that happened? Explain your choice.

7. What was the main point of Arthur's speech? Do you agree that "we can all help make America great by helping others"?

Follow-up Activities

1. Ask students if they can think of other ways that the government honors people. Some examples are giving them medals or awards and creating stamps in their honor. Ask students to think about people they think have done a lot to make America great; they can be famous people or "everyday" citizens. Ask each student to design a stamp that honors the person and shows how they helped to make America great.

2. In your classroom, conduct a contest similar to the contest described in the book. Ask teachers from other classes to judge the essays and arrange for a local dignitary (mayor, president of the school board, city council member, etc.) to visit the class to present awards to the winners.

3. Focus student attention on the monuments and structures that the children in the story visited. Why are these places famous? When we see pictures of them, what do we think about? Assign each child to choose a landmark in our nation's capital or in your state capital and create a poster highlighting the importance of that landmark and how it represents our country.

City Green,
written and illustrated by
DyAnne DiSalvo-Ryan
(New York: William Morrow, 1994).

Summary

When an old building in the neighborhood is torn down because it is unsafe, Miss Rosa and her young friend Marcy decide to put the unsightly empty lot to use as a community garden. With their neighbors, they rent the lot from the city and begin cleaning up the lot and planting seeds. Eventually, even grouchy Old Man Hammer, who once lived in the torn-down building, comes to enjoy the garden.

Initiating Activities

1. Ask students what colors they associate with the city. Post the colors they suggest on the chalkboard. If they suggest green as one of the colors, ask why they chose this color. If they did not choose green, ask why no one mentioned it. Allow time for discussion.

2. Tell students that the title of the book they will be reading is *City Green*. From the cover illustration and the acknowledgments, what do they think might be creating the "green" in the title? Accept all student answers.

Discussion Questions

1. Why was the empty building torn down? Is this a good reason for tearing down a building? What was Old Man Hammer's opinion? Do you agree with him?

2. According to the pictures in the book, what happened to the empty lot after the building was torn down? Have you ever seen an empty lot that got filled up with trash as time passed? Why do you think this happens?

3. What did Marcy and Miss Rosa decide to do with the lot? What did they do to get permission to use the lot? Why was getting a petition a good idea? Do you think a large group of people working together might have be more likely to get the city's approval than just two people? Why or why not?

4. Describe the steps the neighbors went through to turn the empty lot into a community garden. How did the city help?

5. What did Marcy see Old Man Hammer doing at night? Why do you think he planted his seeds at night? What do you think he planted in the garden?

6. What did Old Man Hammer mean when he said, "This lot was good for nothin'. Now it's nothin' but good"? Can you think of something that went from being good for nothing to being nothing but good? What lesson does this story teach us about cooperation?

Follow-up Activities

1. With the class, brainstorm a list of ways in which a community garden would be good for a city neighborhood. Some possibilities include providing fresh food, beautifying the neighborhood, providing a place to sit and enjoy the outdoors or to spend time with neighbors, to give the neighbors something to work on together, and so on.

2. Focus students' attention on Old Man Hammer. Have students generate words that describe Mr. Hammer at the beginning of the book. What accounted for his crankiness? Next, have students generate words that describe Hammer at the end of the book. Why did he change? Help students understand that experiences shape how people behave and that helping others have good experiences can help them become happier and friendlier people.

3. Read the "Starting a Community Garden" section in the back of the book. If appropriate, invite someone from your community who is involved in community gardening to talk to your class about its benefits. With your class, develop a plan for starting a community garden near your school.

A Very Important Day,
by Maggie Rugg Herold,
illustrated by Catherine Stock
(New York: Morrow, 1995).

Summary

On a snowy morning in New York City, families from many countries prepare for a very important event. Not until they arrive at the courthouse downtown does the reader find out that someone in each family is becoming a naturalized citizen on that day. Pride and a sense of celebration mark this "very important day."

Initiating Activities

1. Share with students the title of the book and show the drawing of the calendar on the frontispiece. Ask: What would be a very important day to you—the kind of day you circle in red on your calendar? Accept all student answers.

2. Show students the cover illustration and ask if it gives them any ideas about what the important day in the title might be. Again, accept all answers without indicating whether they are right or wrong. Tell students they will find out whether their answers were right or wrong as they read the book.

Discussion Questions

1. Where does the story take place? Where are the characters in the story from? Does the fact that they are from so many different places suggest why the day is important?

2. Why did Jorge's father think the view from the harbor was the best in the city? Do you think other people would agree with him? What makes a view a good one?

3. Where were all the characters in the book going? What were they doing there? Were any of our predictions about why this was an important day correct? Why was becoming a citizen so important?

4. Reread what the judge said to the people who were becoming citizens. What do you think he meant when he said, "May citizenship enrich your lives as your lives enrich this country"? How does citizenship enrich a person? How does the life of a person enrich the country?

5. Describe some of the ways people celebrated their new country in the story. How would you celebrate becoming a citizen?

Follow-up Activities

1. Encourage students to talk to their parents about their experiences registering to vote and voting. Did they have any difficulties? What are their most memorable experiences?

2. Make other books on voting available to students. Examples are *The Day GoGo Went to Vote* and *Ballot Box Battle* (see annotations on page 17). Conduct a class discussion comparing and contrasting these various efforts to gain the right to vote.

Summary

When a rock crashes through the window of a Jewish family's home in Billings, Montana, they decide to inform people in the community about what happened. Christian ministers, community leaders, and friends of the family decide to take action to show that they oppose such hate crimes. Organizing a campaign to place menorahs in windows all over town, they make a powerful statement against intolerance.

Initiating Activities

1. Tell the students the title of the book the class will be reading and ask if they find anything unusual in the combination of words. If students do not know what a menorah is, point out the picture on the cover and explain that it is a symbol of the Jewish holiday of Hanukkah.

2. Read the subtitle to students and ask them to speculate on what the book might be about. Point out that the dedication of the book gives a clue as to what town is referred to in the subtitle. If students do not know where Billings is, point it out on a U.S. map. You may want to read the "Introduction" to the class before the story is read, although the story may be more engaging if the "Introduction" is read later.

Discussion Questions

1. What made the crash Isaac heard while he was doing his homework? What would you do if you heard a crash while doing your homework? How would you feel? Why do you think someone threw a rock into Isaac's home?

2. What do you think Isaac's mom was talking about when she said, "These terrible people kept threatening and threatening..."? Why won't she tell Isaac what she means?

3. What did Isaac overhear his parents and Chief Inman talking about? What other acts of hate had occurred in Billings? What could Chief Inman, as the police chief, do about the crimes? What did Chief Inman suggest Isaac's family and the community should do about these hate crimes? What would you do if a hate crime took place in your neighborhood?

4. Why do you think Isaac said he didn't want to be a pioneer? Do you think it is hard to be a pioneer? How does being a pioneer help a community?

5. How did Isaac's mom decide to let people in Billings know what happened to the Schnitzer family? Do you think this is a good way to inform people? Can you think of

examples in our community where people have used television to inform others about something that the community needs to stand together against?

6. What happened at the town meeting called by Chief Inman and Margaret MacDonald? Why did Mrs. MacDonald tell the story of King Christian of Denmark? Do you think the group's plan will work? Why or why not?

7. Isaac told his class the story of Hanukkah. What does Hanukkah celebrate? How is the meaning of Hanukkah related to the issue the town of Billings faced?

8. What story did Teresa tell the class? Do you think Teresa's actions in defending her classmate are the actions of a good citizen? Why or why not?

9. How did Isaac feel when he saw the menorahs in windows all over Billings, including the sign in Teresa's window? What do you think the menorahs say about the citizens of Billings? What effect do you think they had on the people who did the hate crimes?

Follow-up Activities

1. With students, make a list of people in the story who were good citizens. For each person listed, write an action that person took that shows he/she is a good citizen. For example, Mrs. Schnitzer informed other people of events in their town, Chief Inman and Mrs. MacDonald organized a town meeting, and so on. When students have completed their list, ask each student to choose one person from the list and write him/her a letter explaining why the class thinks he/she is a good citizen.

2. Read *Molly's Pilgrim*, by Barbara Cohen, illustrated by Michael J. Deraney (New York: Bantam, Doubleday, Dell, 1983), which tells the story of an immigrant girl whose family came to the United States to find religious freedom. Although she lived decades before Isaac, she too struggled with being different from her classmates but came to appreciate those differences when she learned more about them. Discuss with students the difficulties of being different, as well as the importance of religious freedom and the ways in which classmates can help a student who is different feel welcome.

3. *Elijah's Angel,* by Michael J. Rosen, illustrated by Aminah Brenda Lynn Robinson (San Diego: Harcourt Brace, 1992), is a charming story that looks at how people with strongly held religious convictions can respect the traditions of others without compromising their own beliefs. When elderly artist Elijah gives his young Jewish friend Michael a carved angel for Christmas, Michael is afraid his parents will be angry about his Christian symbol. They help Michael accept the gift in the spirit of friendship and suggest that he respond in kind. When Elijah displays Michael's menorah in the window, Michael feels an even stronger connection to his friend. Students who read this book as a follow-up to *The Christmas Menorahs* could create artworks that illustrate the idea of religious tolerance.

Mandela: *From the Life of the South African Statesman*, written and illustrated by Floyd Cooper (New York: Philomel Books, 1996).

Summary

This biography of Nelson Mandela focuses primarily on the years before he was imprisoned. His school days, relationship to his family, and development as an activist are recounted in a manner that conveys the indomitable spirit that allowed him to survive his years in prison and emerge as the nation's leader.

Initiating Activities

1. Ask students to brainstorm what they know about Nelson Mandela. Post their answers on the chalkboard. When they have exhausted their knowledge, ask them to analyze the items you have posted. Have students posted any information about Mandela's childhood? About his schooling? About his work before he was imprisoned?

2. Explain that students will be reading a book about Mandela's early years. Ask students to speculate on how knowing about events in a person's childhood might help us understand their actions as an adult. If appropriate, share an experience from your early life that has helped shape your adult life (e.g., an experience that contributed to your decision to be a teacher).

Discussion Questions:

1. How were the Thembu people governed? Was Chief Hendry's decision in the case of the ox a fair one? Why or why not? How did the case result in Chief Hendry's being dethroned? Do you think the dethroning was fair? Why or why not?

2. Describe some of the things Nelson learned from his father. How do you think what he learned has influenced his adult life?

3. Why do you think the English teacher changed students' names? How would you feel if your teacher decided to change your name on the first day of school?

4. What did Nelson like about school? Are his feelings about school similar to or different from your own?

5. Why was Chief Joyi important to Nelson? How do you think knowing the stories of his people's past affected him? What stories about America's past are important to young people in America? Explain why you chose the stories you did.

6. Describe what happened to Nelson at Clarkeberry Institute and Fort Hare. Based on these experiences, would you have predicted that Nelson would become a national leader? Why or why not?

7. Why did Justice and Nelson run away to Johannesburg? Arranged marriages were an important custom among the Thembu people. Do you think it was right for the two young men to run away because they did not want to marry the women who had been selected for them? What values or beliefs does their decision show were important to them?

8. What do you think the Xhosa saying "People are people through other people" means? How does the saying apply to Nelson's life? How does it apply to your life?

9. Describe the injustices Nelson witnessed in Johannesburg. What did Nelson do to fight injustice? If you were Nelson's son Thembi, how would you feel about your father's actions and the anger white people felt towards him?

10. Do you think Nelson Mandela was guilty of trying to overthrow the state of South Africa? If a government is unjust, should the people try to overthrow it? Give reasons and examples to support your answer.

11. The author of this book uses wind as a metaphor. What does the wind represent in the book? Does this metaphor help you understand Nelson Mandela's life and the changes that have occurred in South Africa during his life?

Follow-up Activities

1. Read the "Author's Note" at the end of the book with students. What characteristics about Nelson Mandela does Floyd Cooper admire? Can students identify other people who have those characteristics?

2. The book is dedicated to Arthur Ashe. Encourage students to learn more about Arthur Ashe to find out why a book about Nelson Mandela would be dedicated to this African American. What characteristics do they have in common?

3. Encourage students to collect articles on Nelson Mandela and on life in South Africa. What problems do South Africans still face? What actions are being taken to solve those problems? With students, create a bulletin board focused on South Africa's efforts to solve their problems.

4. Return to the question of how a person's early life influences his/her decisions in adult life. Ask students to create a "resume" for Nelson Mandela in which they identify at least three early experiences that helped him to become a great leader.

Eagle Song,
by Joseph Bruchac, illustrated by
Dan Andreasen (New York: Dial, 1997).

Summary

Fourth-grader Danny Bigtree feels out of place in his New York City school, where he is the only Native American student. He hopes his classmates will stop teasing him after his father visits the class and tells the story of Aionwahta and the Iroquois League. Still, only when a family crisis prompts Danny to act does he begin to make peace with his nemesis, Tyrone.

Initiating Activities

1. Ask students to imagine that they have just moved from a small town surrounded by fields and woods to a big city. At their old school, all of the students were of the same ethnic group as they are; no one else in the new school is the same ethnic group and other students make fun of them and call them names. How would they feel? What would they do to improve the situation? Allow time for a small- or large-group discussion of these questions.

2. Explain that this is the situation facing the main character in the book students are about to read. Allow students to examine the book for clues as to what ethnic group the main character belongs to. Be sure students discover the Glossary/Pronunciation Guide at the back of the book.

Discussion Questions

1. What are some of the problems Danny is worrying about as he rides home on the subway? How does reading about Danny's problems make you feel? If you were Danny, what would you do about Tyrone and Brad?

2. Describe Danny's family. What evidence can you find that the Bigtrees are a happy family?

3. What obstacles did Aionwahta have to overcome in working for peace among the five nations? What experiences, people, and talents helped him in his efforts? What do you find most admirable about Aionwahta? Explain your choice.

4. In what ways do you think the League of Peace or Iroquois League was like the United States? In what ways was it different?

5. Why do you think Danny's dad told him the story of Aionwahta? After reading the story, do you have any new ideas for Danny to try in dealing with Tyrone and Brad?

6. Why do you think Mr. Bigtree ended his presentation with the saying, "If you believe in peace, then an enemy can become a friend"? Why is this saying important? What does it mean? Can you give examples to support the statement?

7. How do Danny and his mother feel when Mr. Bigtree has to leave for Philadelphia? Do you think the artist does a good job of conveying their feelings in the picture on page 50? Why or why not?

8. On the morning Danny is late for school, why do you think he feels like his "feet are covered with glue"? Draw a picture to show how Danny felt as he walked down the hall to his classroom. What were his hopes? What were his fears? Try to show these hopes and fears in your drawing.

9. Describe what happened to Danny on the playground. Do you think Tyrone hurt Danny on purpose? What clues can you find to support your answer?

10. Why is Chapter 6 titled "Colors"? What are Will's reasons for joining a gang? Do you think these reasons are good ones? Why or why not? Do you think Danny will join a gang? Why or why not?

11. Describe what happened to Mr. Bigtree in Philadelphia. Based on everything that happened in the book, would you describe Mr. Bigtree as a hero? If so, what characteristics make him a hero to you?

12. Why do you think Danny finally decided to confront Tyrone? Would you have done the same thing? Were you surprised by the outcome of his actions? Explain your answers.

Follow-up Activities

1. Encourage students to find out more about the Iroquois League. How was it governed? What values were important to its people? What are the similarities and differences between the United States and the League?

2. Make a display of symbols of the United States around the classroom. Organize the class into small groups and assign each group to find out more about the symbols. What are their origins? Are any others linked to Native American history, legends, or beliefs? On what other sources did the creators of these symbols draw? What are the symbols designed to evoke in citizens of our country?

3. Many people make arguments similar to Will's in explaining why young people join gangs. They say that the gang creates a family or community for young people. Conduct a class discussion in which students consider how young people might be helped to find a community without joining a gang. What actions could our government take? What actions could schools take? What actions could individuals take?

Summary

Eleven-year-old Rosey is a first-generation American living in New York before World War I. As she works on a school assignment to write her family's stories, the reader learns what it means for a Jewish family to "become American" in the early 20th century.

Initiating Activities

1. Read the title of the book aloud to students. Ask them when you might be concerned about whether a word rhymes or not. Does this help them predict something about the book?

2. Read the page preceding the first titled chapter aloud to the group. Discuss with the class how Rosey feels about the new school year and teacher. How does the author convey Rosey's feelings? Have students had similar feelings as a new school year was about to begin? What does the author mean when she says the children of Jewish immigrants "became Americans"? Is anyone who lives in America an American, or does "being American" mean something else?

3. Tell students that as they read the story of Rosey and her family, they will be learning about some values important to her family. Explain that a value is something that a person thinks is important. Some values that many Americans think are important are equality and justice. Ask students to brainstorm some other values. Explain that they will be thinking about values that Americans share—values that make a person a good citizen in a democracy—as they read about Rosey's family "becoming American."

Discussion Questions

(for use after reading the first three chapters)

1. Why do you think Miss Edgecomb spends so much time talking about democracy and being a good citizen? Do you think this has anything to do with "becoming American"? What does Rosey think Miss Edgecomb has forgotten? Do you think it is fair that being born in this country "counts"?

2. What does Miss Edgecomb tell her students to do because it will help them respect themselves? Do you think she is right? Why or why not? What does Rosey mean when she says "Because I am part of my family, knowing my family's stories is part of knowing myself"?

3. What are some of the things that make life in America difficult for Momma? Imagine you are Rosey's mother. How would you feel about life in this new country?

4. What does Rosey mean when she says Uncle Benny and Tante Ruth are very political? Why might Rosey's father think Uncle Benny is "too political"? What does her father think of Uncle Mendel? Based on his reactions to the uncles, what is your opinion of Rosey's father?

5. Have you ever done anything like Rosey did when her baby sister was born? Why do you think Rosey ate all the candy? How do you think she felt? Do you think she learned anything from this experience?

(for use after reading the fourth through eighth chapters)

6. How was Bogdana different from other Polish girls who worked for Rosey's family? What did Bogdana's story help Rosey understand about people who come to America? Do you think people still come here for a dream? Explain your answer.

7. Why do you think Momma is not a storyteller? What does the story of Pyro tell you about Momma? What kind of a person is she? Which of Rosey's parents do you like better— her mother or her father?

8. Do you think Rosey's family members were good friends to the Carnitsky family and to Bogdana and Charlie? Give examples to support your answer. Do you think being a good friend is like being a good citizen? Why or why not?

9. A saying in Rosey's family was "Jokes, not people, are for laughing at." What does this saying mean? What value does it reflect? According to the chapter "Nothing at all," what was another value that was important to Rosey's father? Do you think that kindness and honesty are good values for citizens, as well as family members? Why or why not?

(for use after reading the ninth through twelfth chapters)

10. What does the word *justice* mean to you? Do you think "Justice" is a good title for the story about Yonkeleh and Herschel's rubber band ball? Why or why not?

11. Describe what happened when Rosey and Sadie went to the library. What does this story tell you about the values of the Sachs family? Are patriotism and love of learning good qualities for an American? Why or why not?

12. What is the New York Collegiate Equal Suffrage Vote? How did Rosey's Momma start going to meetings about voting? Why was voting important to her? Is voting part of becoming American? Explain your answer.

13. Think about all of Rosey's stories. Which story did you like best? What did you like about that story? What did it tell you about Rosey's family?

14. What do you now think it means to "become American"? Would becoming American mean the same thing to all immigrants? Do people born in the United States "become American" too? Why or why not?

Follow-up Activities

1. Encourage students to write stories about their own families. You might have them focus on stories that reflect values important to their families or simply write stories that are

often told in their families and then analyze the stories to see if they reflect important values or beliefs.

2. Have the students create a bulletin board entitled "Becoming American." On the bulletin board, they should display pictures, news stories, poems, and other artifacts that reflect values shared by many Americans.

3. Invite a recent immigrant to class to talk with your students. Ask the immigrant to talk about the process of "becoming American." Students whose parents or grandparents are immigrants could interview them about this process. The stories students collect could then be compared to see whether there is a common process of "Americanization" or whether each person's experience is unique.

4. For younger students, another book that explores the process of "becoming American," this time from the perspective of a young Italian-American girl also named Rosey, is *American Too*, by Elisa Bartone, illustrated by Ted Lewin (New York: Lothrop, Lee and Shepard, 1996). Students who could not read *Brooklyn Doesn't Rhyme* should be able to read *American Too*. They could compare the experiences of the two Roseys by role playing a conversation between the two girls or by creating drawings of their similar experiences.

***Stink Bomb Mom*,**
by Martha Freeman
(New York: Delacorte Press, 1996).

Summary

Rory Mudd's mom is, to say the least, unusual. Rory takes solace in her large collection of pets, but it is her dog Agnes who gets her in trouble with the law. Rory and Agnes must execute a daring rescue of the mayor's son to get themselves out of trouble in this humorous story.

Initiating Activities

1. Ask students to list some of the rules they must obey at home. What purposes do these rules serve? What might be some disadvantages of not having such rules?

2. Tell students they are going to be reading a book about a family with very few rules. The title of the book is *Stink Bomb Mom*. What does the title suggest about the book and about the character of the mother? Allow students to speculate briefly on what the book and character will be like.

Discussion Questions

(for use after reading chapters 1-6)

1. What evidence does the first chapter give to show that Rory's family is somewhat unusual? Based on the first chapter, which characters do you like best? Least? Why?

2. Describe Rory's collection of pets. Why do you think she has so many pets? Look for clues as you read the rest of the book. What do the pets and the way Rory cares for them tell you about her?

3. What is the significance of the line, "Sometimes I wonder who's the mother in this outfit"? What does Rory do that a mother usually does? What rules has Rory created for herself to follow? In her situation, what do you think you would do?

4. Describe the events at the Cinnamon Seminar. How might the disaster have been avoided? What was the funniest thing about what happened? What was the saddest thing about what happened? Explain your choices.

(for use after reading chapters 7-12)

5. What do you think of Rory's idea of living with her father? What reasons can you think of for and against the move?

6. What did the letter from the Municipal Court say? What law is the court enforcing? Do you think Rory is being treated differently because the complaint against Agnes came from the Mayor? What is your evidence? Do you think it is fair that Rory has "no recourse"? What would you do in Rory's position?

7. What are some of Doria's ideas for dealing with the letter from the Court? What rights does she suggest using? What are the pros and cons of each idea? Which, if any, would you put into action?

8. What do you think of Mr. Tunnbaum's accusation that Doria is an unfit mother? List the best arguments for Mr. Tunnbaum and for Doria. What suggestions would you make to help Doria become a better parent?

9. Look up the Fourth Amendment to the Constitution. Do you think it applies to Rory's situation? Why or why not?

(for use after reading chapters 13-20)

10. Why does Rory say it's "pouring catastrophes"? Were you surprised that Mr. Tunnbaum left home? Why or why not?

11. Do you think Rory's plan for disguising Agnes will work? What could keep the plan from working?

12. What does Rory do to show she is a good friend to Pookie? What character traits does Rory show?

13. Describe what happened when the Animal Control officers came to Rory's house. Did any of the things that happened surprise you? Could the problems have been avoided? If so, how?

14. How did Rory and Agnes get out of trouble? Do you think this is a realistic resolution to their problem? Did you like this resolution? Why or why not?

15. At the end of the book, why do you think Rory says she and her mother are learning from each other? What can Rory learn from her mother? What can Doria learn from Rory?

Follow-up Activities

1. Assign students in pairs to role play a conversation between Rory and Doria in which they try to establish some rules for their family to follow in the future. Charge students with developing rules that will solve or avoid the problems Rory and Doria faced in the book.

2. Rory's father really doesn't know Rory. Ask students to write letters from Pookie to Mr. Mudd, describing the characteristics that make Rory a good friend and a good person.

3. Encourage students to share the book with their families and to follow up by discussing the reasons their parents have established certain rules for the family.

Summary

Fifth-grader Miata Ramirez and her best friend Ana Avila decide to run for school president and vice president against class clowns Rudy Herrera and Alex Garcia. The girls take a mostly serious approach to the election (although they do get perms because they think curly hair might help their chances) while the boys promise longer recesses and ice cream every day. Throughout the election process, Miata learns a lot about herself and about what it takes to be a leader.

Initiating Activities

1. Share with students the title of the book, _Off and Running_. Ask them to speculate on some of the possible meanings of this title—that is, what might the characters in the book be running toward or for? If no one suggests running for office, suggest this as a possibility and ask students to consider why someone trying to be elected to office is described as "running."

2. Tell students that this book is about fifth-grade students running for school president and vice president. In pairs, have students develop ideas for a campaign for school offices—how would they campaign, what might their issues be, whose support would they seek? Give each pair a sheet of posting paper and a marker for use in sketching a poster that describes one of their ideas. Post their sketches around the classroom. Encourage students to compare their ideas with those of the characters as they read the book _Off and Running_.

Discussion Questions

(for use after reading chapters 1-4)

1. Why did Miata want to be school president? Do you think these are good reasons for running for office? Why was she surprised to learn that Rudy and Alex would be running against Ana and her? Why does she think that the girls and some of the "more intelligent boys" might vote for her instead of for Rudy and Alex?

2. Explain what happened with the autographed baseball. Would you have made the same decisions Miata made? Why or why not?

3. Describe Miata's family. Which family member would you most like to meet? Give reasons for your choice.

4. Make two lists, one showing Miata and Ana's plans if they are elected, the other Rudy and Alex's plans. Whose ideas are better? Why? Whose ideas do you think will be more popular with their classmates? Why?

5. Why did Miata and Ana decide to perm their hair? Do you think it was a good idea? Have you ever had a similar experience?

(for use after reading chapters 5-8)

6. What is your favorite part of the chapters that describe the visit from Senor Gomez the Magnificent and the field trip to the zoo? Give reasons for your choice.

7. Why does Miata want to meet someone important? In what way is Dona Carmen important? How does she help Miata? If you could meet Dona Carmen, what would you ask her about her life?

8. What is a *quinceanera*? What were some of the reasons Miata did not seem to enjoy the *quinceanera*? Can you think of a time when you felt the same way at a party or celebration?

(for use after reading chapters 9-11)

9. Why did so many other students turn up at school with perms? Do you think this means that Miata and Ana will win the election? Why or why not?

10. Describe the chase to recapture Vaca. How did Miata end up in trouble with Mr. Rios again? Do you think her punishment was fair? Why or why not?

11. Do you like Miata's "ideas to help save the world"? Do you think this was a good assignment? What would you write about if your teacher assigned a composition on "Five Simple Ideas to Help Save the World"?

12. Describe how Miata and Ana won the election. Were you surprised to learn that Rudy and Alex voted for Miata and Ana? What would have happened if they had voted for themselves?

13. Who was making the anonymous calls to Miata? Were you surprised when you found out who it was? If you were Miata, what would you have done when you found out who was making the calls?

14. Provide evidence that Miata was a good school president. How does she demonstrate "to all in our country a willingness to get involved"? Why is willingness to get involved important to a democracy?

Follow-up Activities

1. Hold a real or mock class election in your class. Encourage candidates to use what they learned from Miata's experience to develop well-thought-out and feasible campaigns.

2. Gary Soto has written other books featuring Miata and Rudy. Assign students to write a story about one of these characters that illustrates further growth toward becoming good citizens.

3. Create a class survey to determine how many parents, aunts, uncles, grandparents, etc. of students ran for class or school office, whether they won, what they learned from the experience, and so on. Assign each student to survey two adults. Have students pool their data and see what conclusions they can draw from it.

The Great Squirrel Uprising, by Dan Elish, illustrated by Denys Cazet (New York: Orchard, 1992).

Summary

The squirrels are blockading the entrances to New York's Central Park. Soon they are joined by the city's pigeons and birds from up and down the East Coast. Ten-year-old Sally is the only human who understands what the animals want—an end to the litter humans strew around the animals' home. Skateboarding squirrels, a Mozart-loving pigeon, and a doughnut-dependent mayor populate this hilarious story.

Initiating Activities

1. Ask students if they are familiar with the term *uprising*. Help them arrive at a class definition of the term.

2. Next, share the title of the book with the class. Lead a class brainstorm of reasons why squirrels might revolt, encouraging creativity and even silliness.

3. Have students read the list of characters and consider why the author included it. You may want to have students sketch a map of Central Park on the chalkboard so it will be easy to refer to as the class reads the book.

Discussion Questions

(for use after reading chapters 1-4)

1. Imagine the sight Sally saw when she got to the West 72nd Street gateway into Central Park. How would you react to such a sight? How did you react when you read about it?

2. According to Scruff, why were the squirrels taking over the park? Do you think the animals' anger against humans was justified? Why or why not?

3. Describe Scruff, Franklin, and Mort. What role does each one play? Which one is funniest? Which do you like best? Why?

4. How did Sally's parents feel about her helping the animals? Do you think her parents were being reasonable or prejudiced?

(for use after reading chapters 5-8)

5. How does the mayor first react to the squirrel uprising? If you were one of his advisors, what would you tell him to do?

6. How did people take advantage of the uprising? Can you think of a real-life example similar to the way in which people made money selling squirrel merchandise?

7. How did Scruff react to Franklin's idea about using pigeons on the picket lines? Would you say Scruff is prejudiced? Why or why not?

8. Reread Scruff's speeches to his troops. (Dan Elish has him reworking Shakespeare in several places.) What values does he appeal to? Given the conditions, do you think his speeches will be effective?

9. Why does Scruff spend so much time getting his picture taken? Can you think of real-life leaders who do the same thing?

10. What is the reaction when the union of rats offers to help with the blockade? What do the rats want in exchange for their help? What do you think Scruff should do?

11. What caused Franklin to fly away from his friends? Do you think he was right to do so? Why or why not? Do you think power is changing Scruff? Give evidence to support your answer.

(for use after reading chapters 9-12)

12. Describe the scene at the concert. What was the funniest thing that happened?

13. Scruff talks about "a land of the animals, run by the animals, for the animals." Would Scruff be a good leader for such a land? Explain your answer.

14. What seems to be the mayor's biggest concern in trying to end the squirrel uprising? What do you think Dan Elish is saying about government leaders through the way he portrays the mayor? Do you agree with his view?

15. Describe the reasons for Sally to help the mayor, as well as the reasons not to help him. Would you have made the decision Sally made? Why or why not?

16. Describe the agreement that ended the uprising. Evaluate the agreement on a scale of 1 to 5, with 1 being excellent and 5 being poor. Support your rating with reasons.

Follow-up Activities

1. Ask students to select what they thought were the funniest scenes in the book and create illustrations of the scenes. Then encourage students to think of real-life parallels to the scenes they selected and illustrate those as well.

2. Assign students to write their own stories about animal uprisings. What, for example, might classroom animals revolt in order to gain? How could such an uprising be ended?

3. Discuss with the class the use of humor to express one's views on government, people's behavior, or particular issues. Examine how Dan Elish used humor and compare his work with that of other authors, movie or television writers, or political cartoonists.

Seedfolks,
by Paul Fleischman
(New York: HarperCollins, 1997).

Summary

The voices of 13 residents of a Cleveland neighborhood describe how and why they became involved in turning an empty lot into a garden. While their reasons for becoming involved are diverse, their shared interest and activity creates a true community in a rewarding and informative story.

Initiating Activities

1. Ask students if they agree or disagree with the following statement: No event happens only once; an event experienced by three people happens three times. As part of their discussion, ask them to consider how each of them might describe an event that they all experienced. You may want to actually have students write brief descriptions of an event that occurred that day and have a few students share their descriptions. How are the descriptions similar? Different? Tell students that Paul Fleischman is an author who often writes his books using the voices of many different characters.

2. Explain that students will be reading a book by Paul Fleischman called *Seedfolks*. Encourage students to speculate about the meaning of the title.

Discussion Questions

1. Why did Kim decide to plant seeds in the empty lot? What qualities did she want her father to know about? Do you think she picked a good location for her "garden"? Why or why not?

2. Describe the history Ana has seen from her window. How do Ana's suspicions about Kim make you feel? How did she feel when she discovered she was wrong? What does Wendell's story add to your understanding of Ana?

3. Why did Wendell decide to get involved with the garden? Do you think he is right about the things he says he cannot change? Explain your thinking. What was similar and different about Wendell's and Kim's reasons for planting a garden?

4. What does Gonzalo mean when he says, "The older you are, the younger you get when you move to the United States"? Do you think he is right? How does the story support his view? How does the garden change his opinion of Tio Juan?

5. What steps did Leona take to get the trash cleared from the lot? Why do you think it was so hard to get the government to help? Should it be hard to get government help? What do you think of Leona's idea of taking a bag of trash with her to the government office?

6. Describe Sam's occupation. Do you think this is important work? What rules might help avoid the problems Sam described?

7. What do you think of Virgil's father's idea of using the garden to make money? What would you have said to him? Why is Mrs. Fleck important to the story? Do you think it is significant that she is a teacher? Why or why not?

8. What happened to Sae Young to cause her to stop going to her business? Do you think other crime victims would react in the same way? How did the garden help Sae Young?

9. Why did Curtis start growing tomatoes? Even if Lateesha doesn't like him, how has he changed for the better? Do you think he is right in saying that people respect an individual's property more than government property? Do you think this should be true?

10. Describe the way the people of the neighborhood solved the problem of getting water to the garden. What was good about the way in which the people solved the problem?

11. Nora says that a garden is like a soap opera. Leona tells Maricela that she and the garden are both part of the natural system, running on sunlight and water. Which description of a garden do you like best? Why?

12. Describe the cooperation that Amir observed. How did people's attitudes toward each other change as a result of the garden? Do you think these changes made the neighborhood a better place to live? Why or why not?

13. Reread Florence's story about the seedfolks. Who were the seedfolks in her family? How were the neighborhood gardeners like her family's seedfolks? Do you think *Seedfolks* was a good title for the book?

Follow-up Activities

1. Have each student choose a favorite character from the book and write another chapter from that person's perspective, explaining how the community that developed around the garden helped improve his/her life.

2. Ask students to draw illustrations for the book, showing the lot before and after the seedfolks did their work. Challenge them to show through their illustrations as many ways as they can in which the garden helped improve the community.

3. With older students, you might discuss whether a garden is a good metaphor for a functioning community. What characteristics of a good community does a garden have? What other metaphors could be used to convey what a good community is like?

```
┌─────────────────────────────────────────────────────┐
│                                                     │
│              Germy in Charge,                       │
│     by Rebecca C. Jones (New York: Dutton, 1993).   │
│                                                     │
└─────────────────────────────────────────────────────┘
```

Summary

Sixth-grader Jeremy "Germy" Bluett decides to run for student representative on the school board. Elected by the same high school students who voted a boa constrictor homecoming queen, Germy learns about limits on power when he finds himself unable to deliver on his campaign promises (one of which was to begin summer vacation at Thanskgiving). Through a variety of mishaps, he also learns a great deal about the responsibilities involved in holding public office.

Initiating Activities

1. Tell students the title of the book the class will be reading. Ask each student to imagine that his/her name is substituted for "Germy" in the title. What would they like to be in charge of? Why? What kinds of changes would they make if they were in charge of the school, for example?

2. If students have read other books about Jeremy by Rebecca C. Jones, ask them to share what they know about Jeremy. If they have not, tell students that the initial chapters in the book say that Jeremy "had a reputation for making things happen," was known as Germy Blew It, "had been known to forget an assignment or two," and sometimes started things he didn't finish. Does Jeremy sound like the kind of person they think should be "in charge"? Why or why not? What qualities would they look for in a leader?

Discussion Questions

(for use after reading chapters 1-4)

1. What is your first impression of Jeremy? Why do you think the author started the story with Jeremy in bed, not wanting to get up for school? Does that influence how you feel about Jeremy?

2. How did it make Jeremy feel when Margaret quoted Robert Kennedy to him? What do you think the quotation ("Some men see things as they are and say, why; I dream things that never were and say, why not?") means? How did Jeremy's parents react when he repeated the quotation that evening? Why do you think they reacted that way?

3. Why does the author use italics for certain parts of the book? What do these passages lead you to think Jeremy is going to do?

4. Why does Jeremy want to run for the school board? Do you think these are good reasons? What qualities do his parents say are needed to be a good school board member? Does Jeremy have these qualities?

5. What does Mr. Bluett mean when he says he "votes on the issues"? Do you think most people vote on the issues? What issues does Mr. Bluett say students should be interested in? Does Mrs. Bluett seem to agree? How can you tell? Do you agree with Mr. Bluett? Why or why not?

(for use after reading chapters 5-8)

6. According to Margaret, what is a platform? What are some ideas Margaret has for Jeremy's platform? What are some of Jeremy's ideas? Which do you think are better ideas? Which do you think will be most popular with the voters?

7. What problems did Jeremy see at his school? How did he propose to solve the problems? What problem did Squirrel have? What solutions do Jeremy and Squirrel see for this problem?

8. What happened when the Bluetts went to the library? Has anything similar ever happened to you? What did you do? What do you think Jeremy will do about his book report?

9. Describe the argument that Margaret and Jeremy had. What do you think caused the argument? How would you resolve their disagreement?

(for use after reading chapters 9-13)

10. What is the importance of burping and belching to Jeremy and his friends? Why was Jeremy embarrassed about burping instead of belching? How did the girls in his class feel about belching? Have you experienced different attitudes among boys and girls? Do you think these differences are important? Why or why not?

11. Imagine that you and your family were watching the president give a speech about the deficit. How would your family's response be similar to and different from the way Jeremy's family reacted to the speech? How might the president make people more interested in a topic like the deficit? Is it important that people aren't interested?

12. What do you think Mr. Bluett means when he tells Jeremy to "think big"? Do you think Jeremy's "No School at All" idea is a good example of thinking big? Why or why not? Can you think of an example from real life of a person who thinks big? How do you know this person is a "big thinker"?

13. Describe what happened from the time Jeremy got up on Friday morning until he went back to his own school after giving his speech. What, to you, was the funniest thing that happened? Did you feel sorry for Jeremy? Did you feel sorry for Margaret? Why or why not?

(for use after reading chapters 14-18)

14. Were you surprised that Jeremy won the election? Why do you think the high school students voted for him? How does Ms. Morrison explain his election? Do you think she believes the reasons she gives? Why might she say what she does even if she doesn't believe it?

15. How do Jeremy's schoolmates react to his election? What is his response? What do you think will happen when Jeremy tries to solve the problems his schoolmates have complained about?

16. What does Jeremy's mother tell him about campaign promises? Do you think she is right? Give evidence to support your answers.

17. What "terrific idea" does Jeremy have while practicing his signature? Who do you think will like this idea? Who do you predict will not like this idea?

18. Were your predictions about Jeremy's book report accurate? Do you think his solution to the problem will work? Why or why not?

(for use after reading chapters 19-22)

19. Jeremy thinks that he is a "man with power." List some of the ways he tries to use his power. What are the results of his actions? What does this suggest about his power?

20. What are some of the issues before the school board? What are Jeremy's ideas about these issues? Based on Jeremy's ideas and actions since his election, do you agree with Ms. Morrison that a sixth-grader does not belong on the school board? Why or why not?

21. What decision did Jeremy make about staying on or leaving the school board? Do you think it was a good decision? What decision would you have made in his place? Give reasons for your decision.

Follow-up Activities

1. Invite a school board member to class. Prior to the visit, have students prepare questions to ask, based on the book. Some questions might include:

> How were you elected to the board?
> What are some of the issues you have dealt with on the board?
> What are some of your powers as a school board member? What are some things
>   you cannot do to change the schools even as a school board member?
> Does the board have a student representative? Do you think a student representative
>   is a good idea?

2. Ask students to imagine that they will be voting for a student representative for the school board. What qualities would they look for? Ask them to write a paragraph or draw a cartoon illustrating the ideal candidate for student representative to the school board.

3. Discuss with students how adults in the story reacted to the quote from Robert Kennedy. Encourage students to create a mural that illustrates their understanding of the quotation. As an alternative, students could ask adults they know what quotations from leaders inspire them. Students could then create a mural illustrating the quotations they think are the most powerful.

Marian Wright Edelman: Fighting for Children's Rights, by Wendie Old (Springfield, NJ: Enslow, 1995).

Summary

Marian Wright Edelman is a prototypical involved citizen, dedicating her life to public service, particularly to the effort to improve the lives of children. Motivated by an upbringing that stressed that "service is the rent we pay for living" and fueled by her experiences growing up black in the 1940s and by her keen intelligence, Wright has lived her life in a way that epitomizes the term "civic virtue."

Initiating Activities

1. Post several quotations from the book around the classroom. Possible examples include:

- Service is the rent we pay for living.

- We will not be a strong country unless we invest in every one of our children.

- There is no free lunch. Don't feel entitled to anything you don't sweat and struggle for.

- Remember your roots, your history, and the forebears' shoulders on which you stand.

Ask each student to choose one of the quotations and think about what it means. Encourage students to draw or write their interpretations of the quotations selected.

2. Tell students that the quotations are from a woman named Marian Wright Edelman, whose life represents many features of good citizenship. As students read her biography, ask them to look for evidence that Edelman would be a good role model for citizenship.

Discussion Questions

(for use after reading chapters 1-3)

1. How did seeing the poor child in Cleveland, Mississippi, influence Senator Robert Kennedy? Why do you think this child had such a big effect on the senator?

2. Why did Marian Wright decide that she needed to work in Washington, DC? What does that tell you about the role of the U.S. government in solving our nation's problems?

3. Members of Marian Wright's family emphasized "being prepared." What does "being prepared" mean to you? What did it mean to Marian Wright and her family?

4. Describe Marian Wright's childhood. What were some of the rules her parents set for their children? Why do you think they set these rules? Explain whether you think the rules the Wrights used in their home were good or bad rules.

5. Describe some of Marian Wright's childhood experiences with prejudice and Jim Crow. Who helped her succeed despite these experiences? How did these experiences affect her?

(for use after reading chapters 4-6)

6. How was Marian Wright's experience at Spelman College similar to her upbringing in South Carolina? What new experiences at Spelman helped her grow? Why do you think that traveling to the Soviet Union was such an important experience for her?

7. Explain the sit-ins that young African Americans undertook in 1960. Do you think the students who participated in the sit-ins were working for the common good? To improve our democracy? Why or why not?

8. Why did Marian Wright decide to become a lawyer even though she was not interested in the law? Do you think becoming a lawyer was a good decision? Why or why not?

9. How were African Americans prevented from voting in the 1950s and 1960s? What part did Marian Wright play in trying to gain voting rights for black people? How would you have reacted to the situations she described in Greenwood and Jackson, Mississippi?

10. Robert Coles said that Marian Wright had "unwavering moral courage." What do you think he meant? What actions support his description of Ms. Wright?

(for use after reading chapters 7-10)

11. Marian Wright Edelman and her husband raised their children to have certain values. Based on her biography, what do you think those values were? Do you think those values are values important to citizens in a democracy? Why or why not?

12. Why did Marian Wright Edelman establish the Children's Defense Fund? What are its purposes? Describe some of the activities of the CDF. Do you think such an organization is necessary? Do you think such an organization should be necessary? Explain your answer.

13. Pick the CDF poster that you like the best. How does it represent the ideas that Marian Wright Edelman has worked for all of her life?

14. Read Marian Wright Edelman's "Twenty-five Lessons for Life." If Americans followed these lessons, would our democracy be better than it currently is? Why or why not?

15. Make a list of all the things that Marian Wright Edelman has done to promote the common good. Put a star by those that involve the government. Put a check by those that involve businesses. Circle those that involve other kinds of community groups. Based on the list you have created, define the work of a "good citizen."

Follow-up Activities

1. Have students illustrate Marian Wright Edelman's "Twenty-five Lessons for Life" in a series of posters that show how living according to these values/guidelines could improve

our democracy. You might wish to read aloud to students the portions of Edelman's book, *The Measure of Our Success* (Boston: Beacon Press, 1992) that elaborate on the lessons.

2. Encourage students to create graphics that show the influences on Marian Wright Edelman. Use the graphics as the basis for discussing how negative experiences, as well as positive ones, can help motivate people to work for the common good. Encourage students to reflect on their own life experiences in terms of how they might work to prevent any negative experiences they have had from happening to other young people in the future.

3. Assign students to find out more about the Children's Defense Fund and its work. Work with the students to identify a service project they could complete that would help advance the aims of the CDF or of another children's advocacy group.

A Small Civil War,
by John Neufeld (New York: Atheneum, 1996).

Summary

The small town of Owanka erupts in controversy when a group of parents protest inclusion of *The Grapes of Wrath* in the tenth-grade curriculum. The controversy divides families, as eighth-grade firebrand Georgia Van Buren discovers when her father supports those who want the book removed from the schools. Georgia, meanwhile, becomes a leader in the group "Freedom Is Reading Is Freedom" and her older sister Ava struggles with whether to remain an objective reporter or to take a stand on the issue.

Initiating Activities

1. Display several books that have been banned or challenged in schools or libraries. Possibilities that may be familiar to students are *The Prydain Chronicles*, by Lloyd Alexander; *The Little Mermaid*, by Hans Christian Anderson; *Clan of the Cave Bear*, by Jean Auel; *My Brother Sam Is Dead*, by James and Christopher Collier; *A Wrinkle in Time*, by Madeleine L'Engle; *The Chocolate War*, by Robert Cormier; *Forever* and *Are You There God? It's Me Margaret*, by Judy Blume; *Tar Beach*, by Faith Ringgold; *The Haunted Mask*, by R.L. Stine; and *Where the Sidewalk Ends*, by Shel Silverstein. Your school's librarian/media specialist should be able to help you identify several books that have been challenged in schools around the country. Ask students what these books have in common. If no one mentions it, explain that all of these books have been banned or have been suggested for banning.*

2. With the class, identify some reasons why parents or other members of the community might want a book removed from a class reading list or from the school library. Also identify the rights that such removal might conflict with—freedom of expression, freedom of the press, and educators' freedom to teach what they think is important. If time permits, ask students to interview their parents about what conditions, if any, might cause them to raise questions about a book assigned for reading in your class.

3. Explain that the book students are going to read deals with controversy about a book by John Steinbeck called *The Grapes of Wrath* and whether tenth-grade students should read the book in their English classes. Share the title of the book with the class and ask what the use of the term "civil war" suggests about the controversy.

Discussion Questions

(for use after reading chapters 1-8)

---

*The idea for this initiating activity was taken from a lesson developed by Jackie Johnson, Beth Giles, and Judy Schaefer of Campus Middle School, Cherry Creek (CO) Schools, and published in *Education for Freedom: Lessons on the First Amendment for Secondary School Students* (Denver, CO: First Amendment Congress, 1997).

1. What does the author mean when he says that Georgia runs "on emergency power." How does this description help you create an image of Georgia? In what other ways does John Neufeld help you get a picture of Georgia in the very first chapter of the book? Do you think Georgia would be a friend of yours if you went to Owanka Junior High? Why or why not?

2. Describe the difference of opinion between Georgia and Charlotte regarding the town meeting. Which view is closer to your own view of the role of young people in public issues—that you don't vote so adults can ignore you or that your presence makes a difference? Give evidence to support your position.

3. Explain the issue before the city council. Why did Georgia think that Fairchild Brady was making an issue of the book? Explain Stanley Sopwith's objections to the book, as well as Mr. Nagle's arguments in support of students' reading it. What arguments did Georgia and her parents make at dinner following the meeting? Which of the arguments do you think is strongest? If the argument you selected carried the day, what would be the effects, both good and bad?

4. What similarities do you see between Georgia and her sister Ava? What differences?

5. Georgia argues that if the town votes to censor *The Grapes of Wrath*, then the teachers won't be able to do the jobs they have been trained to do. Instead, they will have to teach only what the town agrees on. How much control do teachers have over what is taught? What are the arguments for teacher control? What are the arguments for community control? Has this topic been controversial in your own community?

(for use after reading chapters 9-17)

6. At the second meeting about *The Grapes of Wrath*, what arguments do Mrs. Nichols and Ms. McCandless make? What are the strengths of their arguments? What are the weaknesses? Why do you think Mr. Brady refuses to accept the approach they recommend?

7. What conflicting values make it difficult for Martin Brady to decide which side to support? What conflict is Ava experiencing regarding her role as a reporter? Write a letter to Martin or Ava giving them advice about what they should do.

8. Describe Con Arrand. What does Georgia like about him? How has his life been different from the lives of most young people in Owanka? Would you like to grow up as Con has? Why or why not?

9. Do you think Alva Van Buren is a good mother? Give evidence to support your answer. Do you think Mr. Van Buren is a good father? Give evidence to support your answer.

10. Why did Susan Woods want to meet Ava? Do you agree with her description of the role of newspapers? If you were Ava, would you agree to work with Susan? Why or why not?

(for use after reading chapters 18-24)

11. Read the letters that Georgia and Reverend Fickett wrote to the local newspaper. What values do they appeal to? Do you think their appeal is effective? How could their letters be made more persuasive?

12. Susan Woods says that when an issue comes up, "what it does to people causes the whole argument to expand, to slop over into other issues." What do you think she means by

this? Do you think she is right? Use examples from the book and from the news to support your answer.

13. Ava says that in opening up the censorship issue, "Mr. Brady had opened cellar doors, and candidates for the city council—all running against him—had emerged into the light." What is the author trying to suggest by using the term "cellar doors"? Does Ava think the candidates will be good leaders for the community?

14. Describe the argument between Georgia's parents. How did hearing their parents arguing about the issue affect Georgia and Ava?

15. Why do you think Georgia's friends were "ever so slightly...easing off, easing away"? Have you ever had an experience in which friends became less close because of your views or actions on a controversial issue? How did this experience make you feel? Does the experience seem to affect Georgia? Do you think it affects the way she feels about Con?

(for use after reading chapters 25-32)

16. What did Ava learn through her interview with Mr. Claffin? How was Mr. Claffin affected by the controversy? Do you think most teachers would react in the same way? How did Susan Woods respond to Ava's story about Mr. Claffin? Does her reaction change your feelings about Susan? Why or why not?

17. Describe FIRIF's efforts to influence the election. What words does the author use to suggest that Georgia and her cohorts might be going overboard? How does he also suggest respect for their efforts? On balance, do you think they are doing good work or going overboard?

18. Reread Mr. Bracken's speech to the crowd that gathered for the fund raiser. What was he trying to tell people? Why do you think people got so upset? Why was even Georgia angry about his donating the money to FIRIF? In Mr. Bracken's place, what would you have done?

19. Give examples from the book that show how people exaggerate when they are arguing about a controversial issue. Do you think such exaggeration helps or hurts their efforts to make a point?

(for use after reading chapters 33-41)

20. Explain the events that led to the resignation of Ms. McCandless. Do you think she should have been asked to resign? Do you think she should have resigned when asked to do so? Explain your answers.

21. Describe the argument Martin and Ava had after they saw the movie version of *The Grapes of Wrath*. With whom do you agree? Give reasons for your choice.

22. What do you think finally caused Ava to write the article explaining her own views on the issue? Do you agree with her decision, or do you think she should have remained an "objective" journalist? What would you have done in her position?

23. Why did Alva Van Buren cry after the church members' discussion of the issue? How do the views and feelings of the Van Buren family help you understand how personal and political opinions influence each other?

24. Restate, in your own words, the FIRIF pledge that Georgia asked people at the rally to recite. What values does it include? Do you think these values are important to a democracy? What values important to a democracy might Georgia's opponents claim their side supported?

25. Why do you think the citizens of Owanka voted to remove *The Grapes of Wrath* from the school curriculum but also voted Mr. Brady out of office? What, if anything, does this suggest about how people make voting decisions?

26. Georgia is angry at the end of the book. Describe what you think might happen between Georgia and other members of her family in the weeks following the election. Do you think they can resolve their differences? Can they learn to live with their differences?

Follow-up Activities

1. Students could compare *A Small Civil War* with *Memoirs of a Bookbat,* by Kathryn Lasky (San Diego: Harcourt Brace, 1994), which also deals with people who want to have a say-so in the books students read in school. Lasky's book, however, focuses on the effects on one family whose parents are "migrants for God," moving from town to town to oppose various books in the schools. Their daughter, Harper, is an avid reader who loves many of the books her parents want to censor. By the time she is 14, she feels like her parents' slave and decides that she must take radical action to gain her freedom. The contrast with the Van Buren family, where diverse views may cause arguments and frustration and yet are tolerated, is marked and should prompt lively discussion among students.

2. Choose one of the books that you displayed at the beginning of this lesson. Have students role play a school board meeting in which some parents present reasons for banning the book and others argue for its inclusion. Following presentations of arguments, students selected to role play school board members should discuss and vote on the issue. Following the role play, discuss with students how complicated such issues are. Assign each student to write a brief essay explaining how he/she would vote if he/she were a school board member and the reasons for that vote.

3. With the help of the librarian/media specialist have your class host a Banned Book Night at the school. Students could create a disply of books that have been banned or challenged and put together a panel to discuss issues related to censorship and age-appropriateness. Possible panelists might include a librarian, local author, students, parents, representatives of the clergy, and so on.

4. Have students find out how objections to books are handled in your community. Is this a good way to consider the rights and interests of everyone concerned? How could the process be improved?

Zlata's Diary: A Child's Life in Sarajevo,
by Zlata Filipovic (New York: Viking, 1994).

Summary

Zlata is a happy middle class fifth-grader when war comes to Sarajevo. Her diary chronicles the impact of war—and the loss of freedom that accompanies it—on daily life. Her reflections on "the kids," as she calls the politicians, provide interesting fodder for discussion of appropriate roles for political leaders.

Initiating Activities

1. Read students the title and subtitle of the book and ask them to share what they know about Sarajevo. Find Sarajevo on a map and point out that it is part of an area that has changed rapidly in the 1990s and has seen much conflict. If possible, bring in some newspaper articles about current events in Sarajevo/Bosnia-Herzegovina.

2. Tell students that some people have called Zlata Filipovic the Anne Frank of Sarajevo. If students are not familiar with Anne Frank's story, provide a sketch of her life and the diary that she kept. Ask them to speculate on what Zlata might be recording in her diary if she is considered the new Anne Frank. You may wish to reassure students that Zlata is not killed (or may make that information available by reading the book's "Introduction" aloud with the class).

Discussion Questions

(for use after reading diary entries through April 1992)

1. Describe Zlata's life as she describes it in her diary entries during the fall months of 1991. What surprises you about her description? How is her life similar to your own life? How is it different?

2. What leads Zlata to say "I don't understand politics" (entry for October 22)? Have you ever felt the same way about events in the "real world" that have affected your own life?

3. How does the war in Dubrovnik affect Zlata's family? What actions do they take to help people in that city?

4. Describe the events that took place in Sarajevo in March 1992. How did these events affect Zlata and her family? Do you think it is true that "you can't hide all the bad things that are happening from us children" (entry for March 24)? Provide evidence to support your answer. How does knowing about "bad things" affect children?

5. How does Zlata refer to the politicians? What does use of this word show about people's attitudes toward politicians? Do you think the attitudes of people in Bosnia-Herzegovina are similar to attitudes of people in the United States? Why or why not?

6. Reread the entry for April 12. Explain this entry: "I keep thinking about the march I joined today. It's bigger and stronger than war. That's why it will win. The people must be the ones to win, not the war, because war has nothing to do with humanity." Do you agree with Zlata? Why or why not?

(for use after reading diary entries through August 1992)

7. Describe the events that led Zlata to write: "I'M SO MAD I WANT TO SCREAM AND BREAK EVERYTHING" (entry for May 13, 1992). Do you think you would react in the same way to the events in Sarajevo if they happened in your town? Why or why not?

8. What rights or freedoms has Zlata lost because of the war? Do you think loss of freedoms is inevitable in wartime? Why or why not?

9. What is the importance of Radio France Internationale? Why is news from outside the country important to the people of Sarajevo? Do you think the press is especially important during wartime? Why or why not?

10. Reread Zlata's diary entry for June 18, 1992. How has her thinking about politics changed since the war first started? How would you explain the changes in her thinking?

11. According to Zlata's diary, what is the United Nations' role in the war? In what ways is the UN helping the people of Sarajevo? What other actions is the UN considering?

(for use after reading diary entries through December 1992)

12. How did Zlata's family try to continue their family traditions in spite of the war? What adaptations did they have to make? Why might maintaining traditions be important in wartime?

13. Reread Zlata's diary entry for October 1. Explain this quotation: "The 'kids' are negotiating. Will they finally negotiate something? Are they thinking about us when they negotiate, or are they just trying to outwit each other, and leave us to our fate?" What attitudes about leaders does this quotation reflect? Do leaders most often think about the people or about outwitting each other? Provide evidence to support your answer. What evidence later in the diary helps you determine whether the leaders of the sides in this conflict thought about the people?

14. Throughout her diary, Zlata writes about the pros and cons of leaving Sarajevo. What are the pros? What are the cons? If you were Zlata, would you want to stay or leave? What is the most persuasive reason for your decision?

15. On November 19, Zlata writes of her understanding of the "politics" causing the war. Describe her views of the causes of the war. Do you agree or disagree with her views? Give reasons to support your answer.

(for use after reading diary entries through June 1993)

16. Why do letters bring both joy and tears? Have you ever had an experience that made you both happy and sad at the same time?

17. Why are journalists visiting Zlata? What do you think the effects of her diary's being published and news stories about her appearing in newspapers and on television in other countries might be? Consider the effects on Zlata, on her family, and on her country.

18. Compare a typical day in Zlata's life in May 1993 with a typical day in September 1991. Does her life in 1993 still have any similarities with your own life? What accounts for the similarities or lack of similarities?

19. Find some passages that provide evidence of Zlata's growing sadness. Do particular events cause the sadness, or do you think it is the cumulative effect of the war and loss of freedom and security it entails? What do you think will happen to Zlata?

(for use after completing the book)

20. Reread the entry for July 17, 1993, paying special attention to the "message" Zlata gave at the promotion for her book. What is the meaning of her message? What is she telling the "kids" responsible for the war? What is she telling the people of the world?

21. Zlata says that Sarajevo is "slowly ceasing to be what it was" (see diary entry for September 19, 1993). Why does she say this? What changes would have to occur before you said your city was no longer itself?

22. Zlata describes her life as a "closed circle." What does she mean by this?

23. Has Zlata's attitude toward the "kids" changed by the end of the book? Why does she find it impossible to hope that the war can end?

24. In the last diary entry, Zlata says "I keep thinking that we're alone in this hell, that nobody is thinking of us, nobody is offering us a helping hand. But there are people who are thinking about us." How can people in other countries help those living in nations where war is occurring? What are some reasons why other countries should or should not take action to end a war in which they are not involved?

Follow-up Activities

1. Have students write letters to Zlata (Zlata loved getting mail from American pen pals). In their letters, students should focus on what they learned by reading Zlata's diary.

2. Encourage able readers to read *The Diary of Anne Frank* and compare and contrast the experiences of the two young women.

3. Assign students to find newspaper or newsmagazine articles about the events Zlata described in her diary. How are the accounts similar and different? What do the news articles indicate that United Nations and United States officials were saying and doing about these events?

```
┌─────────────────────────────────────────────────────────┐
│  ┌───────────────────────────────────────────────────┐  │
│  │                                                   │  │
│  │              Rio Grande Stories,                  │  │
│  │              by Carolyn Meyer                     │  │
│  │       (San Diego: Gulliver Books, 1994).          │  │
│  │                                                   │  │
│  └───────────────────────────────────────────────────┘  │
└─────────────────────────────────────────────────────────┘
```

Summary

Seventh-graders in an Albuquerque middle school are looking for a fund-raising project when they hit upon the idea of creating a book that reflects the diverse heritage of their community. As the students work on their chapters, they learn more about their own heritage, as well as the values that hold the community together. Their product not only raises money, it is a service to the entire school community and a source of great pride. Meyer intermixes chapters about the students' lives with their contributions to the class project in a way that is entertaining and adds to the reader's understanding of the richness of this diverse community.

Initiating Activities

1. Share with students the title of the book and ask them to find the Rio Grande on a map. What communities are located along the river? (Don't forget those on the Mexican side.) What do students know about the history of the area and about the people who live there? Allow time for students to share their knowledge.

2. Read "A Note from the Author" with the class. How does Carolyn Meyer feel about New Mexico? Based on this introductory note, what kinds of stories do students think will be included in *Rio Grande Stories*? Have students examine the table of contents and the pronunciation guides at the back of the book for clues as to the book's contents.

Discussion Questions

(for use after reading the stories of Jeremy Steinberg, Tony Martínez, and Pauline Romero)

1. What was the Heritage Project? How would students benefit from researching how their "family history fit into the history of the United States"? Would you apply to be in such a program? Why or why not?

2. Describe the idea the students in the Heritage Project adopted as their way of contributing to the school sculpture. What were Jeremy's and Rosa's qualifications for being editor of the book? Who do you think was better qualified? How would you rate the class solution to the problem: excellent, good, fair, or poor? Give reasons to support your rating.

3. Who were the "Hidden Jews" of New Mexico? How did being a "hidden Jew" affect Mrs. Naomi Luna? Does this story influence your thinking about religious freedom? Why or why not?

4. Why was Padre Martínez a hero to Tony? What qualities do you think make someone a hero? Why did Ms. Kelsey criticize Tony's choice of Padre Martínez as his topic? Why did Teresa stick up for Tony? What would you have recommended that Tony do?

5. What do you think Pauline's Aunt Helen meant when she said "I tell you that my whole life is about making a pot"? How does Pauline's story illustrate what Aunt Helen means? How did Pauline decide to become a potter? Imagine that someone told you they were going to buy something you made every year so they would have a big collection when you became famous. How would this make you feel?

(for use after reading the stories of Teresa Chávez, April Ellis, and Tomás Jaramillo)

6. What were some of the things the students did not like about Ms. Kelsey? Do you think their dislike was justified? Make up a list of qualifications for substitute teacher in Rio Grande Middle School. Would the list be different for a substitute teacher in your school? Do you think Teresa "cured" Ms. Kelsey? Why or why not?

7. What values were important to April's parents? What values were important to her grandparents? Whose values were most like those of a majority of people? How did the different values of her parents make April feel? What happened when Tom, her father, volunteered at school? Were you surprised at what happened at the end of her story? Why or why not?

8. Why was Tomás embarrassed to be from Española? Is their a community in your state that people make jokes about? Why do you think people pick on one community like this? What would you do if you were the mayor of a town that everyone makes fun of?

9. Describe Tomás's contribution to the book. Why did he call it "Española Joke"? Do you think that was a good title? Why or why not?

(for use after reading the stories of Franklyn and Jacquelyn Cox, Ricky Begay, and Rebecca Rivera and Sara McGinley)

10. Describe the Coxes' Thanksgiving potluck dinner, including the people, the food, and the conversation. What, to you, was the most interesting part of the dinner? Give reasons for your choice.

11. Why were Estabanico and Georgia O'Keeffe important to Franklyn and Jacquelyn? Do you see any similarities between these two people that help you understand any similarities between the twins? What about differences?

12. What was Ricky's contribution to the book? What do you think Ricky learned from watching his grandfather make jewelry and talk about his work? What do you think Ricky learned from watching his grandfather interact with people at the Old Town Plaza?

13. How did Ricky's grandfather serve his country in World War II? What was especially surprising or interesting about Mr. Bennett's story?

14. Explain some of the ways that Sara and Rebecca were different. What allowed them to be best friends despite their differences? How did the people in Sara and Rebecca's neighborhood all work together to get ready for *Las Posadas*? Do you think you would like to live in their neighborhood? Why or why not?

(for use after reading the stories of Rosa Gonzales, Peter Kingston and Joey Baca, and Manuel Medina)

15. How many different versions of the story of *La Llorona* are told in the chapter about Rosa? Can you think of a story that you have heard many different versions of? How do you think different versions of a story get started? Why do you think the story of *La Llorona* was important to the Hispanic people in the book?

16. Reread Rosa's "Tortilla History." How does the tortilla represent a uniquely American food? What values could you say are represented by the tortilla? Be sure to consider Mr. Gonzales's story about the rich man and the poor man.

17. Describe the pilgrimage from Santa Fe to Chimayó. Why did Joey's father and grandfather make the pilgrimage? Why do you think Peter decided he would make the pilgrimage again next year?

18. How did Peter and Joey contrast Chimayó and Los Alamos? What does the contrast show you about the state of New Mexico? What towns in your own state could provide a similar contrast? What would the contrast tell others about your state?

19. Make a list of the things Manuel worried about after joining the Heritage Project. Imagine yourself in his position. Would you have worried about these same things? What would you have done in Manuel's position? Do you think he will worry about so many things in the future? Why or why not?

20. Mrs. Salazar said the theme of the sculpture being created for the school would be "the river and how it connects people through time and across cultures." How does the Heritage Project book help you understand this theme? What do you think a sculpture with this theme might look like? Make some sketches of your own ideas and discuss them with your classmates.

Follow-up Activities

1. Ask students to design a cover for the book created by the Heritage Project students. Encourage them to show, through their designs, how diversity enriched the community. Students could also write a "blurb" to go on the back of the book. What would they say to capture the book's meaning and to encourage people to read it?

2. Organize a book-writing project focused on the heritage of your community. What kinds of diversity are represented in your community? What shared values hold your community together? What special knowledge or skill is passed down from generation to generation in your students' families? What interesting historical events or people could students research? If the project develops successfully, you may wish to arrange for the book's publication and sale to benefit a school or community project selected by the students.

```
┌─────────────────────────────────────────────┐
│                                             │
│              The Bomb,                       │
│           by Theodore Taylor                 │
│     (San Diego: Harcourt Brace, 1995).       │
│                                             │
└─────────────────────────────────────────────┘
```

Summary

Set on the island of Bikini, this novel begins in March 1944, as Americans are about to liberate the island from the Japanese. Over the next few years, however, the Americans also bring trouble to the island's residents, including teenager Sorry Rinamu, as they choose the Bikini Atoll as a test site for atomic weapons. Sorry decides to take desperate action to try to stop the bombing that he believes will destroy his home land forever.

Initiating Activities

1. Share with students the title of the book and lead a class brainstorm of what students know about the development of the atomic bomb. Post the information students provide, suggesting that they will have the opportunity to check the accuracy of this information and add to it as they read Theodore Taylor's novel. You may want to draw a timeline on the chalkboard and have students post historical information as they glean it from the novel.

2. Explain that the book is set on the island of Bikini. Locate Bikini on a world map and ask if students know how the bomb and this remote area in the Pacific Ocean are related to each other. Allow students to speculate.

Discussion Questions

(for use after reading Book I)

1. Describe a typical day on the island of Bikini. How did the war change island life? In what ways did life stay the same, even though Bikini was affected by the war? Why were the people of Bikini happy to see American planes, boats, and men?

2. Explain how the residents of Bikini governed their community. What might be some good points of this form of government? What might be some of its shortcomings?

3. Based on what she teaches, what values are important to Tara Malolo? What is your evidence? Why did Sorry like Tara so much?

4. Why is Sorry so interested in the Japanese magazine he found? What does it represent to him? What does he like about the magazine? What is puzzling to him? Have you ever had a similar experience when introduced to an artifact from another culture?

5. How does reading the between-chapter history of nuclear weapons affect you as a reader? Why do you think the author included that information? Why did he choose to include it in the way that he did?

6. What is the significance of the albatross? What omens or signs of bad luck are common in our culture? How do people react to these signs?

7. Describe Abram Makaoliej, Sorry's uncle. How does his return to the island affect Sorry? Why do you think Abram decided not to kill the tiger shark that gave him his scar? Would you have done the same thing in his position? Why or why not?

8. How did Sorry and Abram react to the bombing of Hiroshima? What questions does Sorry have? What questions do you have?

(for use after reading chapters 1-7 of Book II)

9. How are Books I and II different? How does Theodore Taylor let you know right away that Book II will be different? What do you predict will happen in Book II?

10. Why did the United States choose Bikini for its atomic weapons test site? Do you think it would have chosen a site whose residents were U.S. citizens? Why or why not? What rights of citizens might be violated by such a relocation? Can you think of other examples of relocations in U.S. history? How are these examples similar to and different from the situation of the people on Bikini?

11. How did the Americans try to convince the people of Bikini that testing atomic weapons on their island was a good idea? What arguments did they make? What values did they appeal to? How did they use the people's own system of government to help them? If the families had voted not to move, what do you think the United States would have done?

12. Where did the people of Bikini decide to move to? What were some good things about Rongerik? What were its bad points? How do you think life will change for the people of Bikini when they move to Rongerik?

13. Describe Abram's plan for stopping the testing. What rights is he using? Do you think he is being a good citizen? Why or why not?

(for use after reading chapters 8-14 of Book II)

14. In what ways did people protest the bombing? Whose views of the protests are closer to your own—Tara's or Chief Juda's? What other disagreements do the two have? What values account for their differing views?

15. List some of the scientific questions Dr. Garrison said would be studied. Do you think answering these questions is a good justification for conducting tests of the bomb? Why or why not? What do you think Dr. Garrison meant when he told Sorry, "One part of me agrees with you. But the scientific part doesn't."

16. Describe the scene as the islanders left their home. Pick one character and describe the thoughts he/she might have been having as they left.

17. What did Tara mean when she said reporters had "Hawaiian disease." Do you think reporters today sometimes fail to look below the surface? How does it affect what they write about? Give examples to support your answer.

18. Why did Sorry decide to take over Abram's protest? Why did Tara and Jonjen decide to go? Do you think their protest will be successful? Imagine that you are a member of the village council. What would you say to Sorry?

(for use after reading Book III and the factual epilogue)

19. Given the results of the bombing and of the protest, do you think the protest served a useful purpose? Why or why not?

20. What values were in conflict in this novel? How should decisions involving such value conflicts be made? What should the role of the people, the government, and scientists be in making such decisions?

Follow-up Activities

1. Have students design a memorial to Sorry, Tara, and Jonjen. Begin by discussing with students the purposes of a memorial. Brainstorm with students some criteria for deciding whether a design for a memorial is a good one. Examples of criteria might be that the memorial is visually appealing, reflects the values of the people it is dedicated to, and educates people who visit it. Let students work in small groups to design memorials and then encourage them to evaluate the designs using the class-developed criteria.

2. Point out that people in government—like all people—can make bad decisions. They are often influenced by values or ideas that seem important or are popular at a particular point in history but later are revealed to be injust or less important than they seemed. This story illustrates two kinds of bad decisions that have been made by government—decisions about relocating people (e.g., Trail of Tears, Japanese-American internment camps) and decisions about uses of atomic power/radiation (e.g., radiation experiments conducted on retarded children or sick people). Encourage students to research these areas and to develop suggestions for avoiding these types of bad decisions in the future. Possibilities include strengthening checks and balances and making sure that the people are well educated and involved in monitoring government actions.

THEMATIC UNITS, CHILDREN'S LITERATURE, AND CITIZENSHIP

Introduction

The three units that follow are intended to serve as models for ways in which works of children's literature can serve as the centerpiece or the stimulant for interdisciplinary units that develop understandings related to civics and government. The units are flexible, requiring as few as three class periods to complete but expandable to fill as many as ten. They blend literature/language arts and citizenship with other subject matter and skills.

The first unit, "Freedom of Expression," focuses primarily on the many ways in which people express themselves, using literature to illustrate forms of expression and the importance of expression to people. The unit very briefly introduces the idea that freedom of expression is an important right protected by the First Amendment.

As its title suggests, "What Makes a Good Citizen? Models in Literature," invites students to expand their understanding of what constitutes citizenship. By analyzing the actions of literary characters—young and old, past and present—students develop descriptions of the characteristics of a good citizen. They share their thinking through a simulated interview program in which characters from several books exchange views on citizenship.

The final unit, "Equal and Equitable: What's the Difference?", uses Kurt Vonnegut's futuristic short story, "Harrison Bergeron," to stimulate discussion of the relationships among the concepts of *equality*, *equity*, and *diversity*. The activities and discussions are largely open-ended and conducted in small groups to give students the opportunity to develop their own understandings in a setting that encourages all to participate.

Freedom of Expression

Unit Overview

This unit introduces the concept of expression, using something students have all experienced—birthdays. By examining forms of expression in literature, students become aware of the variety of ways in which people communicate their ideas, needs, and feelings and begin to recognize how important expression is to people. They are then introduced to the idea that free expression is a fundamental right protected by the First Amendment.

Civic Understandings: At the end of this unit, students will be able to:

- Give a simple definition of expression.

- List examples of different forms of expression.

- Create a form of expression.

- Recognize that freedom of expression is protected by the First Amendment.

Grade Level: K-4

Time Required: 3-4 class periods

Materials and Preparation: Read through the lesson plan and decide what books you will use in presenting the lesson. You may have your own favorite books that will illustrate forms of expression; several that we recommend are:

How Do You Say It Today, Jesse Bear?, by Nancy White Carlstrom (New York: Macmillan, 1992), grades K-2. Every month of the year, Jesse Bear finds a new way to express what he feels. The broad range of ways he finds to say "I love you" should help students understand what is meant by forms of expression. We strongly recommend using this book to introduce the concept of expression to younger students.

Our People, by Angela Shelf Medearis (New York: Atheneum, 1994), grades K-2. A young girl's father tells her about the history of African-American people. The stories provide inspiration for the young girl's dreams, movingly reminding us of the power of stories.

Diego, by Jonah Winter (New York: Alfred Knopf, 1991), grades K-2. With text in both English and Spanish, this simple biography of muralist Diego Rivera shows how his love of painting and of the people of Mexico combined to create a unique form of expression.

Adapted from *Education for Freedom*, a curriculum published by the First Amendment Congress at the University of Denver.

The Storyteller, by Joan Weisman (New York: Rizzoli, 1993), grades K-3. A young Native American girl finds herself in the city far from her home in Cochiti Pueblo, missing her friends and especially her story-telling grandfather. As she strikes up a friendship with an elderly Anglo woman, she learns that sharing stories with friends of many ages and backgrounds creates a new and caring community in the city.

Sato and the Elephants, by Juanita Havill and Jean and Mou-sien Tseng (New York: Lothrop, Lee and Shepard Books, 1993), grades K-3. The title character is a Japanese artist—a carver of ivory. One day, he discovers a bullet embedded in the piece of ivory he is carving. Suddenly, he realizes that an elephant died to provide the material he carves. He expresses his feelings by deciding to become a carver of stone instead.

Frederick, by Leo Lionni (New York: Knopf, 1967), grades K-4. While the other mice gather supplies for the winter, Frederick seems to dream away the summer. When winter comes and all the food is gone, however, the other mice are grateful to Frederick, who helps them forget their hunger by reciting the poems he created. The theme of art and its ability to sustain us is presented with grace and style.

Teammates, by Peter Golenbock (San Diego: Gulliver Books, 1990), grades 2-4. This book tells the story of Jackie Robinson's difficulties as the first African American to play major league baseball. A courageous example of the use of freedom of expression is provided by fellow Dodger Peewee Reese, who speaks out on behalf of Robinson in the face of hostile ballplayers and fans.

Dinner at Aunt Connie's House, by Faith Ringgold (New York: Hyperion Books, 1993), grades 3-4. Two young people discover a surprising series of paintings of African-American women. What is surprising about the paintings? They can talk, sharing ideas about history. The notion that paintings can speak (albeit not as literally as in the story) is a powerful one for young students to consider as they learn about expression.

From Miss Ida's Porch, by Sandra Belton (New York: Four Winds Press, 1993), grades 3-4. In this charming story, neighbors of all ages sit on Miss Ida's porch and share stories. On this particular night, elders recount stories of brushes with history, including a visit by Duke Ellington's orchestra and Marian Anderson's concert at the Lincoln Memorial. The narrator of the story is a young girl who finds security in the sharing and pride in the stories told.

While we have suggested grade levels for the books, they are simply suggestions; we recognize that individual teachers know the interests and skills of their students best.

A selection of birthday cards would be useful in opening the lesson. You will also need art supplies for the expression project to be done by students, whether making posters, bumper stickers, buttons, or decorated T-shirts. You may wish to coordinate this portion of the activity with the art teacher.

Procedure

1. Display several birthday cards in a prominent place in the room. Ask students why we send birthday cards. (To wish the person a happy birthday, to show the person we care about him or her) What are some other ways in which we wish people "Happy Birthday"? (Say it, sing it, send a telegram, give a gift, have a party, give a hug) Tell students that these are all ways of expressing our feelings about the person's birthday. **Note:** If there are stu-

dents in your class who do not celebrate birthdays for religious reasons, you may skip step 1.

2. Write the word *Expression* on the chalkboard and explain that expression means telling our thoughts or feelings or sharing information. Ask students to brainstorm a list of ways we tell our thoughts or feelings and share information. Post students' responses on the chalkboard under the Expression heading. Some possibilities include talking; writing letters, stories, poems, articles, etc.; drawing a picture or cartoon; making a movie or television program; singing or playing a musical instrument; carying a protest sign; and so on. **Note:** With older students, you may want to skip to step 4 after the brainstorming.

3. Read the book *How Do You Say It Today, Jesse Bear?* aloud with students. After each set of three months, stop and ask what forms of expression Jesse used in those months and add them to your chalkboard list. After you have read all 12 months, ask students what they think "it" is; what is Jesse saying in all these different ways? Allow them to speculate and then finish reading the story. Discuss the story, encouraging students to comment on the forms of expression that appeal most strongly to them.

4. Ask students to give examples from their own experiences of the forms of expression listed on the chalkboard, as well as other forms of expression. When students have listed a number of examples, assign them to look for additional examples during the rest of the school day and at home that evening. You may have each student bring in an example to class the next day.

5. At the beginning of the next class period, ask how many students observed or brought in examples of each of the forms of expression listed on the chalkboard. Tally the results and allow some time for students to share observed examples.

6. Depending on the age and abilities of your students, you may proceed in one of two ways:

A. For younger students, students who are less able readers, or students who have trouble working independently, have the entire class focus on a single book, either the Jesse Bear story read the previous day or another age-appropriate book; *Frederick* would be a good choice for any grade level. If you choose a new story, read it aloud with the class and identify the form of expression that is important in the story. Discuss why that form of expression was so important.

Next, divide the class into small groups and provide students with the materials needed to produce a form of expression; all groups may work on the same form (such as a bumper sticker) or groups can choose their own forms (bumper stickers, posters, greeting cards, buttons, poems, skits, songs, etc.). Their products should answer the question: Why was telling thoughts or feelings or sharing information important in this story?

For example, if you decide to use the Jesse Bear book, you might form groups based on the months of the year in which students' birthdays occur (two months per group) and assign each group those months from the book. The group assigned March and April may decide to make a kite that says "When you know someone loves you, you can fly."

B. For older students or a class with able readers and independent workers, you may divide the class into groups first and give each group a different book to read. Each group's task is to:

- Read their book.

- Identify a form of expression in the book and discuss why it is important to the story.

- Create a form of expression that answers the question: why was expression (telling thoughts or feelings or sharing information) important in this story?

For example, a group that reads *Dinner at Aunt Connie's House* would identify art as a form of expression and discuss how the art helped inform Melody and Lonnie and made them feel proud of their heritage. The group might then create a poster captioned "Art Says It All" and illustrated with events important to group members.

As students work, circulate among the groups, making sure that students are focusing on expression and its importance. Because many of the books raise other interesting issues, you may need to assure students that they will have time to explore these issues as well.

7. Allow time for sharing and discussion of the group work, focusing particularly on the importance of expression.

8. Ask students to imagine that they have an important idea. They cannot tell anyone else about it, write about it, or in any other way express their idea. How would they feel? What would they do? What problems would be created? Allow time for discussion of student reactions to this scenario.

9. Tell students that in the United States, such a problem should not happen because we have a right to freedom of expression. Ask students if they know what *right* means. Help them arrive at a simple definition of the term. Such a definition might be *"Having a right means being able to do something without anyone saying that you can't."* Thus, having the right to freedom of expression means being able to tell your thoughts or feelings without someone stopping you. The right to freedom of expression is protected by the First Amendment to the Constitution.

Extension

1. Create a "Forms of Expression" bulletin board using the students' expression projects. Encourage children to bring in additional samples of expression to display. One way to garner additional examples is by reading more books with students. For example, if you did not use all the books listed in the **Materials and Preparation** section in the lesson, you may want to make them available for additional reading or read and discuss them with students during "Read Aloud" sessions. For each book read, students can add a new element to the bulletin board, showing the form of expression that was important in the story. To illustrate, if you use the book *The Storyteller* in this fashion, students could draw a Pueblo storyteller doll to be displayed on the bulletin board.

2. Of course, many other books can be used to expand understanding of expression. A book that links directly to the lesson's discussion of ways to say "Happy Birthday" is Susan Pearson's *Happy Birthday, Grampie* (New York: Dial, 1987), in which a girl prepares a special birthday card for her blind grandfather. The power of stories to developing self-identity and a sense of community is a theme in many children's books. Examples include *Mrs. Katz and Tush*, by Patricia Polacco (New York: Bantam, 1992); *Aunt Flossie's Hats (and Crab Cakes Later)*, by Elizabeth Fitzgerald Howard (New York: Clarion, 1991); and *The Rag Coat*, by Lauren Mills (Boston: Little, Brown, 1991). Art as a means of conveying important ideas can be explored further by reading a biography of the author/artist of *Dinner at Aunt Connie's House*. *Faith Ringgold*, by Robyn Montana Turner (Boston: Little, Brown, 1993), is illustrated with Ringgold's unique art works.

What Makes a Good Citizen? Models in Literature

Unit Overview

Often, young people think of citizenship as involving only such activities as holding public office, voting, or serving on a jury. Yet good citizens also contribute to the common good in a wide variety of other ways. Literature provides a rich array of models of promoting the common good, models that this unit draws upon. Following a brainstorm on what makes a good citizen, students analyze characters from literature to determine why they are good citizens. They then take part in a "talk show" in which their characters exchange ideas about citizenship. The unit concludes with students drawing posters that show their ideas of what constitutes a good citizen.

Civic Understandings: At the end of this unit, students will be able to:

- Identify ways in which citizens contribute to the common good.

- Recognize characters from literature who contribute to the common good.

- Create a profile of a good citizen.

Grade Level: 3-6

Time Required: 3-4 class periods (depending on grade level and books selected, additional reading time may be required)

Materials and Preparation: You will need copies of Handout 1 for all students, as well as materials for making posters. You will also need copies of several books that provide models of citizenship. Several that we recommend are described below; the books annotated are generally arranged from easiest to most difficult to read. Biographies could also be used effectively in this unit.

Just a Dream, written and illustrated by Chris Van Allsburg (Boston: Houghton Mifflin, 1990), grade 3. Young Walter is careless, littering and refusing to sort the trash for recycling. When he dreams about a future created by actions like his own, he decides to change his ways. The next night, he dreams about a very different—and much more pleasant—future.

Washing the Willow Tree Loon, by Jacqueline Briggs Martin, illustrated by Nancy Carpenter (New York: Simon and Schuster), grade 3. This book recounts the efforts of ordinary citizens who join together to rescue birds caught in an oil spill. Following the rescue of one bird, a loon that lives in a willow tree, the book's creators show how painstaking the work is, as well as how important and rewarding.

A Day's Work, by Eve Bunting, illustrated by Ronald Himler (New York: Clarion Books, 1994); grade 3. Young Francisco finds work for himself and his grandfather, but the work involves gardening, something they know nothing about. After a long day of work, they discover they have pulled up the plants instead of the weeds. When his grandfather insists that they correct the mistake, Francisco gets a lesson in important values and renewed respect for his grandfather.

The Story of Ruby Bridges, by Robert Coles, illustrated by George Ford (New York: Scholastic, 1995), grades 3-4. Ruby Bridges was a first-grader when she became a pioneer, the first black child to attend an all-white school in New Orleans. Guided by her family, her faith, and a courage beyond her years, she continued attending school, even when she had to pass a mob on her way into the building.

Teammates, by Peter Golenbock, illustrated by Paul Bacon (San Diego: Harcourt Brace Jovanovich, 1990), grades 3-4. This book tells the story of how Jackie Robinson came to be the first African American player in Major League Baseball, as well as what life was like for him in his early days with the Brooklyn Dodgers. The book also highlights the actions of Peewee Reese, who stuck up for Robinson when other players and fans heaped abuse on him.

Freedom's Children: Young Civil Rights Activists Tell Their Stories, edited by Ellen Levine (New York: Avon, 1994), grades 4-6. Editor Levine presents powerful excerpts from interviews with 30 African Americans who were active as young people in the civil rights movement of the 1950s and 1960s. These stories provide a window into both the positive and negative legacies of race relations in our country. They also stand as evidence that young people can make a difference.

Checking on the Moon, by Jenny Davis (New York: Orchard Books, 1991), grades 4-6. This book recounts the events of one summer in the life of Cab Jones. Cab and her older brother have been sent to stay with their grandmother near Pittsburgh while their mother tours Europe with her new husband, a concert pianist. Crime on the street becomes a neighborhood issue, and the neighbors band together to fight, through neighborhood walks and a vigil.

Just Like Martin, by Ossie Davis (New York: Simon and Schuster, 1992), grades 5-6. This book recounts the story of a young African American boy who wants to emulate Martin Luther King by participating in the civil rights movement and being nonviolent. The child's father, who served in Korea, feels that nonviolence won't work and fears his son will be hurt if he participates in demonstrations. Despite the restrictions placed on him by his father, young Stone finds a variety of ways to help his community.

The Unsinkable Molly Malone, by Mary Anderson (San Diego: Harcourt Brace Jovanovich, 1991), grades 5-6. Molly Malone is an unusual 16-year-old. Not only does she supplement her family income by selling her artwork on the street and take social and economic issues so seriously that many of her friends do not understand her, she also gives art lessons to children in a homeless hotel. When two of her young students suffer traumas, she decides that she must do more to help them. She also discovers that while some people think she is too serious, others admire and respect her for who she is.

The Weirdo, by Theodore Taylor (Orlando, FL: Harcourt Brace Jovanovich, 1991), grade 6. This book is the story of Samantha Sanders and Chip Clewt, who work together to solve two murders and to extend a federal ban on hunting bears in the Powhatan, a National Wildlife Refuge. Their efforts include preparing posters, discussing their views at a public meeting, and providing testimony before government officials.

Procedure

1. Open the lesson by writing the following question on the chalkboard: What makes a good citizen? Brainstorm with students characteristics of a good citizen or actions that they think a good citizen would take. Post their answers on the chalkboard or on posting paper.

2. Tell students that some experts have given the following definition of a good citizen:

> A good citizen works for the common good and to protect and improve our democracy.

Help students understand this definition and allow time for them to react to it.

3. Explain that students will be reading several books. While reading, they are going to think about what characters in the books, if any, are good citizens. Depending on the age and reading skills of your students, you may want to have small groups of students read different books or you may want to read several of the books aloud to the class and then organize the students into groups, assigning one book to each group. Distribute Handout 1 to the groups and ask them to pick a character from the book who they think was a good citizen. They should then use the handout to analyze why he/she was a good citizen. Allow time for groups to complete their handouts.

4. Next, tell students that the characters they picked are going to be taking part in a "talk show" or "interview program" on the question: What makes a good citizen? Each person has been nominated to appear on this program, representing good citizens. Ask each group to choose someone to role play their character; as a group, they should prepare an opening statement for the program, focusing on their own answer to the topic question. Students who do not role play the characters will be audience members and will be able to ask questions of all the participants.

5. Set up the classroom so that the guests are facing the audience, with the teacher, as host, in the center or standing in the audience. Begin the simulated program by letting all the "special guests" make their opening statements. Then open the floor for questions. The teacher, as the host, may want to ask questions that help develop the ideas of the common good and how someone can work to protect or improve our democracy. Another possible focus is the idea that someone does not have to be perfect to be a good citizen. Conclude the program while the discussion is still lively.

6. Return to the brainstormed list that students created at the beginning of the unit, pointing out how some of the ideas have been further developed through the group discussions and the simulated talk show. Assign each group of students to use the experiences from this unit—the brainstorm, the reading and group discussion, and the talk show—to create a poster that shows the "Model Citizen." The model might be created from the parts of characters who took part in the talk show; for example, a group might want their "Model Citizen" to have the heart of Ruby Bridges, the gentle hands of the barber who cleaned the willow tree loon, the feet of marchers in the civil rights movement, and so on. When groups have completed their posters, display them around the room or in the school hallways where other classes can enjoy them.

What Makes a Good Citizen?

Some experts say a good citizen is a person who works for the common good and tries to protect and improve our democracy. Think about the characters in your book. Were any of them good citizens?

1. With your group, pick a character from your book. Pick someone your group members think was a good citizen. You will probably have to spend time talking about different characters before you decide. Which character did you pick?_____

2. List some things that this person did to promote the common good. That means they did something to make life better for all people, not just themselves.

3. List some things this person did to protect or improve our democracy. That means they did things to make our country work better.

4. Did the person do anything that a good citizen would not do? If so, list those things here.

5. Using what you have written above, write one or two sentences explaining why you think this character was a good citizen.

Equal and Equitable: What's the Difference?

Unit Overview

"All men are created equal." So states the U.S. Declaration of Independence. These five simple words are the essence of our democracy. But what of our forebears' meaning and intention when they crafted that sentence? The debate continues, and individual interpretations create misunderstandings as well as shared meanings daily in both our personal and professional lives.

Very young students learn to measure fairness with things being equal: "She got more candy than me. That's not fair!" for example. By adolescence, this idea has become more sophisticated: "He gets to stay out later than I do. That's not fair! We're all created equal, aren't we?" Teenagers hear their teachers and parents say, "We want our decision to be equitable for both/all of you." But frequently the decision, while fair, all things considered, is not equal, so that hard feelings, anger, and resentment result—all because students do not understand the difference between *equal* and *equitable*. *Equal* means "the same as; alike in quantity, degree, value; same in rank, ability, merit," while *equitable* means "fair" or "impartial."

Sometimes, students can develop deeper understandings by taking a concept to the outer limits of its literal meaning through rich discussions and experiences. As the concept's meaning deepens for students, they transfer their understanding to other issues in the larger context, and the concept takes on greater and more constructive significance. The fundamental premise "All men are created equal" can be approached in this way. Having a clear working definition of *equal* and *equitable* will provide students with greater insight into the concept of diversity and the issues inherent to it.

Literature is one of the more effective ways of making a point. Everyone loves a good story, and "Harrison Bergeron," the core of this unit, is a good story.

Civic Understandings: At the end of this unit, students will be able to:

1. Explain the difference between the concepts of *equal* and *equitable.*

2. Describe the possible ramifications of legal interpretation when it is taken to its literal limits.

3. Interpret societal trends and predict possible future outcomes.

4. Apply new learnings to current diversity issues as manifested in their schools.

Developed by Helene Willis. Adapted from *Update on Law-Related Education* 19, no. 1 (Winter 1995), pp. 22-24. © 1995 American Bar Association. Reprinted by permission.

5-10 class periods

Material and Preparation: You will need copies of "Harrison Bergeron," by Kurt Vonnegut, Jr. (Handout 2).

Procedure

1. Ask each student to write a definition of each term—*equal* and *equitable*—and then pair up with a partner, compare definitions, and write definitions satisfactory to both. Then have pairs team up in groups of four to share their revised definitions and formulate new ones, which they will write on large chart paper and tape to the wall. After all definitions have been shared with the entire class, facilitate a class discussion about how all the definitions for each term can be synthesized into one. Have the class do so, and use these two definitions as a framework for the continuing lesson.

Do not correct misconceptions and erroneous definitions. By the end of the lesson, which has evaluative as well as diagnostic aspects, students will have revisited and revised the definitions as necessary, based on what they have learned throughout the process.

2. Prior to hearing the short story, students will need some experience with the statement "All men are created equal," primarily to gain an understanding of how individual interpretations of the phrase differ. The activity's outcome will be shared meanings, focused on the interpretive continuum from literal to subjective.

Put the statement on the chalkboard or a bulletin board. Have students go on a hunt to find the text where it appears. Make a copy of the Declaration of Rights from the Declaration of Independence, once this document has been identified as the source document. Enlarge the copy and have a student highlight the statement. Put the copy on a bulletin board.

3. Organize students into groups of three or four. Have them devise questions they would ask the signers of the Declaration of Independence if they were alive. Compile the questions into a master list. As a facilitator and class member, you may contribute questions to the list, such as these: What, if any, influence does this statement have on the laws of our nation? What was the signers' intent? Have interpretations changed over the years since the Declaration of Independence was written? If so, why and how? (Give examples.) What is the literal meaning? How does literal differ from subjective?

Have students devise ways for finding "answers" to questions on the list after they have discussed and shared their personal opinions. Each group may choose a strategy and then follow through, reporting back when done. (One strategy may be to interview a number of people on one or more questions and compile the information into a statistical report to be used later for making predictions, identifying trends, and measuring societal attitudes and perceptions.)

4. For the greatest impact, read aloud to the class the short story "Harrison Bergeron." Have each student write a reaction to the story. Call on volunteers to share their reactions. Ask each student to write one to three questions, issues, or ideas that come to mind and that would lead to a rich group discussion. Get one question from each student; any overlap is fine.

Questions the teacher might contribute include: What does this story illustrate about the rules and laws we live by? How like fiction is this story in today's context? How can we ensure reasonable, consistent interpretations of our laws over time—or can we? If all people are equal in this story, how is it that there is a handicapper general who is obviously not equal to everyone else? How would this story change if she were as "equal" as the others?

5. Decide as a class which five or six questions, issues, and/or ideas are the most interesting and most apt to lead to rich discussions. Have each student select the one that he or she wishes to discuss. Divide the class into discussion groups according to students' choices. Have students conduct their discussions, and afterward have one member of each group report significant points to the class. There may be one or more topics that students want to pursue further as an entire class.

6. Have students substitute *equitably* in the Declaration of Rights. Ask how it reads now. Have students rewrite the short story to the outer limits of the literal interpretation of that statement. The rewrite may be in any genre, including essay, poetry, drama, or newspaper or magazine article. Have students share their rewrites and analyze the differences.

7. Have students identify school rule or policy issues that involve interpretations of *equal* and *equitable*, looking for trends that might suggest a movement toward extremes. Have the class write recommendations for ensuring that all school community members, however diverse, will be treated equitably.

Extension

1. Invite an attorney to your classroom to discuss how various laws are based on the premise, "All men are created equal." Have him or her discuss particular cases in which interpretations of *equal* and/or *equitably* were fundamental to the outcome.

2. Have students look for the words *equal* (*equality, equally*) and *equitable* (*equity, equitably*) in everyday usage, such as in *home equity* or *equal opportunity employer*. Discuss what these and other phrases mean in light of students' understandings of the words.

3. Have students select a proposed or existing law and write a story illustrating what might happen if that law is taken to its literal extreme.

4. There is a wealth of literature that speaks to issues involving equality and equity and the ramifications of taking a given law or rule to its extreme. One of the most provocative is *The Giver* by Lois Lowry (Boston: Houghton Mifflin, 1993). This is an excellent book for the class to read and compare to the short story in the lesson. Current practices in our society that reflect what is happening in the book can lead to discussion on trends and predictions for the future, ideas for change, and involvement as a citizen of our nation and the world community.

Harrison Bergeron
A short story exploring concepts of equality

Kurt Vonnegut

The year was 2081, and everybody was finally equal. They weren't only equal before God and the law. They were equal every which way. Nobody was smarter than anybody else. Nobody was better looking than anybody else. Nobody was stronger or quicker than anybody else. All this equality was due to the 211th, 212th, and 213th Amendments to the Constitution, and to the unceasing vigilance of agents of the United States Handicapper General.

Some things about living still weren't quite right, though. April, for instance, still drove people crazy by not being springtime. And it was in that clammy month that the H-G men took George and Hazel Bergeron's fourteen-year-old son, Harrison, away.

It was tragic, all right, but George and Hazel couldn't think about it very hard. Hazel had a perfectly average intelligence, which meant she couldn't think about anything except in short bursts. And George, while his intelligence was way above normal, had a little mental handicap radio in his ear. He was required by law to wear it at all times. It was tuned to a government transmitter. Every 20 seconds or so, the transmitter would send out some sharp noise to keep people like George from taking unfair advantage of their brains.

George and Hazel were watching television. There were tears on Hazel's cheeks, but she'd forgotten for the moment what they were about.

On the television screen were ballerinas.

A buzzer sounded in George's head. His thoughts fled in panic, like bandits from a burglar alarm.

"That was a real pretty dance, that dance they just did," said Hazel.

"Huh?" said George.

"That dance—it was nice," said Hazel.

"Yup," said George. He tried to think a little about the ballerinas. They weren't really very good—no better than anybody else would have been, anyway. They were burdened with sashweights and bags of birdshot, and their faces were masked, so that no one, seeing a free and graceful gesture or a pretty face, would feel like something the cat drug in. George was toying with the vague notion that maybe dancers shouldn't be handicapped. But he didn't get very far with it before another noise in his ear radio scattered his thoughts.

George winced. So did two out of the eight ballerinas.

Hazel saw him wince. Having no mental handicap herself, she had to ask George what the latest sound had been.

"Sounded like somebody hitting a milk bottle with a ball peen hammer," said George.

"I'd think it would be real interesting, hearing all the different sounds," said Hazel, a little envious. "All the things they think up."

"Um," said George.

"Only, if I was Handicapper General, you know what I would do?" said Hazel. Hazel, as a matter of fact, bore a strong resemblance to the Handicapper General, a woman named Diana Moon Glampers. "If I was Diana Moon Glampers," said Hazel, "I'd have chimes on Sunday—just chimes. Kind of in honor of religion."

"I could think, if it was just chimes," said George.

"Well—maybe make 'em real loud," said Hazel. "I think I'd make a good Handicapper General."

"Good as anybody else," said George.

"Who knows better'n I do what normal is?" said Hazel.

"Right," said George. He began to think glimmeringly about his abnormal son who was now in jail, about Harrison, but a 21-gun salute in his head stopped that.

"Boy!" said Hazel. "That was a doozy, wasn't it?"

It was such a doozy that George was white and trembling, and tears stood on the rims of his red eyes. Two of the eight ballerinas had collapsed to the studio floor, were holding their temples.

"All of a sudden you look so tired," said Hazel. "Why don't you stretch out on the sofa, so's you can rest your handicap bag on the pillows, honey-bunch." She was referring to the 47 pounds of birdshot in a canvas bag, which was padlocked around George's neck. "Go on and rest the bag for a little while," she said. "I don't care if you're not equal to me for a while."

George weighed the bag with his hands. "I don't mind it," he said. "I don't notice it any more. It's just a part of me."

"You been so tired lately—kind of wore out," said Hazel. "If there was just some way we could make a little hole in the bottom of the bag, and just take out a few of them lead balls. Just a few."

"Two years in prison and $2,000 fine for every ball I took out," said George. "I don't call that a bargain."

"If you could just take a few out when you came home from work," said Hazel. "I mean—you don't compete with anybody around here. You just set around."

"If I tried to get away with it," said George, "Then other people'd get away with it—and pretty soon we'd be right back to the dark ages again, with everybody competing against everybody else. You wouldn't like that, would you?"

"I'd hate it," said Hazel.

"There you are," said George. "The minute people start cheating on laws, what do you think happens to society?"

If Hazel hadn't been able to come up with an answer to this question, George couldn't have supplied one. A siren was going off in his head.

"Reckon it'd fall all apart," said Hazel.

"What would?" said George blankly.

"Society," said Hazel uncertainly. "Wasn't that what you just said?"

"Who knows?" said George.

The television program was suddenly interrupted for a news bulletin. It wasn't clear at first as to what the bulletin was about, since the announcer, like all announcers, had a serious speech impediment. For about half a minute, and in a state of high excitement, the announcer tried to say, "Ladies and gentlemen—"

He finally gave up, handed the bulletin to a ballerina to read.

"That's all right—" Hazel said of the announcer, "he tried. That's the big thing. He tried to do the best he could with what God gave him. He should get a nice raise for trying so hard."

"Ladies and gentlemen—" said the ballerina, reading the bulletin. She must have been extraordinarily beautiful, because the mask she wore was hideous. And it was easy to see that she was the strongest and most graceful of all the dancers, for her handicap bags were as big as those worn by 200-pound men.

And she had to apologize at once for her voice, which was a very unfair voice for a woman to use. Her voice was a warm, luminous, timeless melody. "Excuse me—" she said, and she began again, making her voice absolutely uncompetitive.

"Harrison Bergeron, age 14," she said in a grackle squawk, "has just escaped from jail, where he was held on suspicion of plotting to overthrow the government. He is a genius and an athlete, is under-handicapped, and should be regarded as extremely dangerous."

A police photograph of Harrison Bergeron was flashed on the screen—upside down, then sideways, upside down again, then right side up. The picture showed the full length of Harrison against a background calibrated in feet and inches. He was exactly seven feet tall.

The rest of Harrison's appearance was Halloween and hardware. Nobody had ever borne heavier handicaps. He had outgrown hindrances faster than the H-G men could think them up. Instead of a little ear radio for a mental handicap, he wore a tremendous pair of earphones, and spectacles with thick wavy lenses. The spectacles were intended to make him not only half blind, but to give him whanging headaches besides.

Scrap metal was hung all over him. Ordinarily, there was a certain symmetry, a military neatness to the handicaps issued to strong people, but Harrison looked like a walking junkyard. In the race of life, Harrison carried 300 pounds.

And to offset his good looks, the H-G men required that he wear at all times a red rubber ball for a nose, keep his eyebrows shaved off, and cover his even white teeth with black caps at snaggle-tooth random.

"If you see this boy," said the ballerina, "do not—I repeat, do not—try to reason with him."

There was the shriek of a door being torn from its hinges.

Screams and barking cries of consternation came from the television set. The photograph of Harrison Bergeron on the screen jumped again and again, as though dancing to the tune of an earthquake.

George Bergeron correctly identified the earthquake, and well he might have—for many was the time his own home had danced to the same crashing tune. "My god—" said George, "that must be Harrison!"

The realization was blasted from his mind instantly by the sound of an automobile collision in his head.

When George could open his eyes again the photograph of Harrison was gone. A living, breathing Harrison filled the screen.

Clanking, clownish, and huge, Harrison stood in the center of the studio. The knob of the uprooted studio door was still in his hand. Ballerinas, technicians, musicians, and announcers cowered on their knees before him, expecting to die.

"I am the Emperor!" cried Harrison. "Do you hear? I am the Emperor! Everybody must do what I say at once!" He stamped his foot and the studio shook.

"Even as I stand here—" he bellowed, "crippled, hobbled, sickened—I am a greater ruler than any man who ever lived! Now watch me become what I can become!"

Harrison tore the straps of his handicap harness like wet tissue paper, tore straps guaranteed to support 5,000 pounds.

Harrison's scrap-iron handicaps crashed to the floor.

Harrison thrust his thumbs under the bar of the padlock that secured his head harness. The bar snapped like celery. Harrison smashed his headphones and spectacles against the wall.

He flung away his rubber-ball nose, revealed a man that would have awed Thor, the god of thunder.

"I shall now select my Empress!" he said, looking down on the cowering people. "Let the first woman who dares rise to her feet claim her mate and her throne!"

A moment passed, and then a ballerina arose, swaying like a willow.

Harrison plucked the mental handicap from her ear, snapped off her physical handicaps with marvelous delicacy. Last of all, he removed her mask.

She was blindingly beautiful.

"Now—" said Harrison, taking her hand, "shall we show the people the meaning of the word dance? Music!" he commanded.

The musicians scrambled back into their chairs, and Harrison stripped them of their handicaps, too. "Play your best," he told them, "and I'll make you barons and dukes and earls."

The music began. It was normal at first—cheap, silly, false. But Harrison snatched two musicians from their chairs, waved them like batons as he sang the music as he wanted it played. He slammed them back onto their chairs.

The music began again and was much improved.

Harrison and his Empress merely listened to the music for a while—listened gravely, as though synchronizing their heartbeats with it.

They shifted their weights to their toes.

Harrison placed his big hands on the girl's tiny waist, letting her sense the weightlessness that would soon be hers.

And then, in an explosion of joy and grace, into the air they sprang!

Not only were the laws of the land abandoned, but the law of gravity and the laws of motion as well.

They reeled, whirled, swiveled, flounced, capered, gamboled, and spun.

They leaped like deer on the moon.

The studio ceiling was 30 feet high, but each leap brought the dancers nearer to it.

It became their obvious intention to kiss the ceiling.

They kissed it.

And then, neutralizing gravity with love and pure will, they remained suspended in air inches below the ceiling, and they kissed each other for a long, long time.

It was then that Diana Moon Glampers, the Handicapper General, came into the studio with a double-barreled 10-gauge shotgun. She fired twice, and the Emperor and the Empress were dead before they hit the floor.

Diana Moon Glampers loaded the gun again. She aimed at the musicians and told them they had 10 seconds to get their handicaps back on.

It was then that the Bergerons' television tube burned out.

Hazel turned to comment about the blackout to George. But George had gone out into the kitchen for a can of beer.

George came back in with the beer, paused while a handicap signal shook him up. And then he sat down again. "You been crying?" he said to Hazel.

"Yup," she said.

"What about?" he said.

"I forget," she said. "Something real sad on television."

"What was it?" he said.

"It's all kind of mixed up in my mind," said Hazel.

"Forget sad things," said George.

"I always do," said Hazel.

"That's my girl," said George. He winced. There was the sound of a riveting gun in his head.

"Gee—I could tell that one was a doozy," said Hazel.

"You can say that again," said George.

"Gee—" said Hazel, "I could tell that one was a doozy."

INDEX OF BOOK TITLES